Common Ground

ROWMAN & LITTLEFIELD PUBLISHERS, INC.

Published in the United States of America
by Rowman & Littlefield Publishers, Inc.
4720 Boston Way, Lanham, Maryland 20700

3 Henrietta Street
London WC2E 8LU, England

British Cataloging in Publication Information Available

Library of Congress Cataloging-in-Publication Data

Geores, Martha.
Common ground : the struggle for ownership of the Black Hills
National Forest / Martha E. Geores.
p.   cm
Includes bibliographical references and index.
1. Black Hills National Forest (S.D. and Wyo.)—History. 2. Black
Hills National Forest (S.D. and Wyo.)—Management — History.
3. Commons—Black Hills National Forest (S.D. and Wyo.)—History.
4. Forest reserves—Multiple use—Black Hills National Forest (S.D.
and Wyo.)—History.   I. Title.
SD428.B53G46   1996   333.75'17'097839—dc20   95-26263   CIP

ISBN 0-8476-8119-X (cloth:alk.paper)
ISBN 0-8476-8120-3 (pbk:alk.paper)
Printed in the United States of America

♾ ™ The paper used in this publication meets the minimum requirements of
American National Standard for Information Sciences—Permanence of
Paper for Printed Library Materials, ANSI Z39.48–1984.

Common Ground
The Struggle for
Ownership of the
Black Hills National Forest

Martha E. Geores

Rowman & Littlefield Publishers, Inc.

in response to both human action and natural events. This history of the Black Hills National Forest (see Fig 1, location map of the Black Hills National Forest) examines the role of resource definition in the sustainability of a U. S. National Forest as a multiple-use, renewable resource.

The term "sustainable" does not have a standard meaning; its meaning depends on the context in which it is used. For example, the Forest Service uses the term "sustained yield" to refer to timber harvest budgets that allow the annual cutting of only as much timber as is balanced by annual growth (Duthie 1928). This yield is well below the maximum possible yield if sustainability were not a consideration. The concept of a sustainable timber yield is different from the concept of a sustainable multiple-use environment because the former refers to only one resource element, i.e. timber, while the latter considers many resource elements and their interrelationships. Sustained yield timber harvest may be one element in maintaining a sustainable multiple-use forest. In both instances the term "sustainable" implies continued existence.

The concept of sustainable economic development incorporates many of the elements examined here. Again, scholars have not agreed

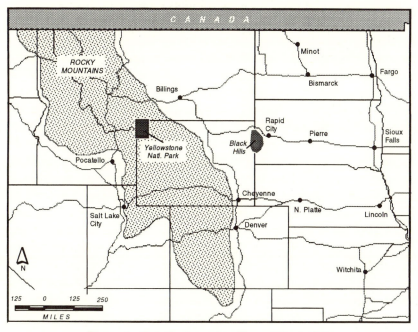

Figure 1. Relative Location Map of Black Hills

Chapter 1

The Black Hills National Forest Is More Than Trees

National forests embody all of the difficult problems associated with renewable natural resources. They confront us with the dilemma of how to manage renewable natural resources in a way that both maximizes their use and preserves their integrity in a sustainable manner. Conservation, preservation, and renewability are all words presently associated with forests worldwide. In national forests the problem is compounded by questions of ownership, rights to use the forests and their products, and the inherent multiple-use nature of all forests.

Natural resources have long been the basis of economic development schemes (Todaro 1989; Leonard 1987), and the use of forests for economic development is hardly a new concept, but it is very much a present concern. That current attention focuses on sustainable use bears witness to the lessons learned from economic development through depletion of potentially renewable natural resources (Allen and Barnes 1985).

Forests are appreciated as renewable natural resources, valued for the use of their products and for their role in maintaining watersheds, soil fertility, and air quality, as well as for their importance as cultural resources in both religious and aesthetic ways. This recognition of the multiple roles of forests did not develop in a vacuum. Most often the multiple role of a forest has been acknowledged only when the forest either disappears or is severely degraded after it has been mined for only one resource element, such as timber. The sustainable-use problem is particularly acute for forests because although their elements are renewable, a forest changes dramatically as an ecological system

1

Contents

Illustrations

Acknowledgments

This book represents the maturing of my dissertation. I am grateful to the many people who helped me start it and who helped me complete it. I owe special thanks to Robert Mitchell, Professor of Geography at the University of Maryland at College Park, for shepherding the book's publication and for his invaluable advice on how to turn a dissertation into a book that people may want to read. Allen Eney's artistic creativity and infusion of enthusiasm are obvious in many of the illustrations and are gratefully acknowledged. All geographers like maps, but not all geographers are skilled at making them. Frank Lindsay created figures 1 and 2 with great competence and good humor. Figures 3 and 5 are the work of Kevin Patrick and are only part of the Patrick family's contribution to this project. Kevin, Theresa, Katie, and Veronica have been with me since the beginning of the journey and I thank them for all of the ways in which they enrich my life, but especially for Mr. Chess.

My dissertation committee at the University of North Carolina should recognize some of their impact on this book, even though the title has changed again. I thank my adviser Stephen S. Birdsall for opening the door to my journey as a geographer, helping me choose my path, and gently guiding me along the way; my foster adviser John Florin, for listening to my Black Hills stories; and Wil Gesler, Peter Uhlenberg, and Tom Whitmore who approved the dissertation. I received dissertation funding from the J. D. Eyre Fund of the UNC-Chapel Hill Department of Geography, the Otis Paul Starkey Fund of the Association of American Geographers, and a National Research Service Award through the Carolina Population Center. Last, but not least, I thank Jennifer Ruark, acquisitions editor at Rowman & Littlefield, for sharing in this project.

The Black Hills are a very special place. It is my hope that all who read this book will view both the Black Hills and other National Forests a little differently.

on a definition of the term "sustainable," but review of several definitions places the Black Hills clearly within the literature on sustainable development of natural resources. Repetto (1985:10) says that the "core idea of sustainability . . . is the concept that future generations should not damage prospects for maintaining or improving living standards in the future." He cautions that sustainable development does not demand "preservation of natural resources or any particular mix of human, physical, and natural assets" because as "development proceeds, the composition of the underlying asset base changes" (ibid.). He also notes that some changes in the asset base are irreversible and biodiversity may be important enough to override economic development goals, but ethical or scientific reasons may be included specifically in a sustainable development plan.

Repetto's analysis is helpful because the Black Hills have been a central element in the economic development of western South Dakota. They contain the majority of the natural resources available in that region and the asset base has changed in the course of economic development. Repetto's concept that development is sustainable, if it does not foreclose prospects for future generations, fits well within the multiple-use sustainability analysis.

In the early 1970s environmentalists insisted that sustainable use included only use that preserved all known forms of plant and animal life. Turner (1988) contrasts this preservationist definition of sustainability with the currently popular sustainable growth model that views the environment in functional, utilitarian terms. Conservation of any plant or animal is only one of several goals to be weighed along with social and economic goals. Not foreclosing options for economic or social uses has become more important than preserving biodiversity as an end in itself (Rees 1990:436). The international sustainable development literature accepts the sustainable growth model, with intentional reference to the merits of maintaining biodiversity and the continued functioning of complex ecosystems (Ascher and Healy 1990:10). Here, "sustainable use of the national forest" means preserving the potential for multiple uses, not necessarily the preservation of any particular version of a use. The term "sustainable" signifies use of the forest and forest products in a way that does not diminish the value of the forest for multiple uses, keeping in mind that not all uses can be quantified in economic terms. Within the context of a functional, utilitarian view of natural resources and potential uses, economic and cultural resources are both considered valuable.

Controversy over the Public Domain

At the heart of the controversy over ownership and control of national forests is an even more basic controversy over whether there should be a public domain and if so, how it should be managed. Arguments over the public domain have occupied federalists and state's rights advocates since the beginning of this nation. Feelings about the issue run more deeply in the West because western lands were designated as part of the public domain as they were acquired by treaties and purchases, while eastern lands tended to be more privately owned from colonial days. This is still a current issue today, although it is now cast in conservation and environmental policy terms as well as state's rights. Cawley (1993) describes the current Sagebrush Rebellion involving land in the public domain in several western states. When all was said and done the rebellion was about whether states or the federal government would control use of land. The argument was much broader than arid sagebrush land, and really widened to include all federal restraints applied to land within states. National Forests were and are very much a part of that argument, although the Black Hills National Forest did not participate in the rebellion.

The history of federal land in the American West poignantly illustrates both the historical process (Clawson and Held 1957) and the contemporary (Cawley 1993) processes. As part of the Old West, the story of the Black Hills embodies the concepts of frontier, settlement, resource extraction, federal ownership, and cultural battleground, as well as the birth and continuing life of a National Forest. The Black Hills region was resettled by new Euro-Americans later than much of the West because it was not until 1874 that the first official foray of new Americans into the Black Hills occurred. The reason for the Black Hills' late entry is that they were recognized as belonging to the Sioux Indian Nation, officially by Treaty of 1868 (Lazarus 1991). Still, their history includes all of the elements of the public domain debates.

By 1879 Congress was acutely aware that it needed to do an inventory of the public lands and passed "The Act of March 3, 1879, relating to Public Lands in the Western Portion of the United States and to the Operation of Existing Laws." The report of the Public Lands Commission was entitled "Use and Abuse of America's Natural Resources" (Bruchey 1972). This comprehensive report detailed the condition and disposition of lands in the public domain. Because so much of the West was public domain and so few people lived there, settlers developed very proprietary and parochial attitudes about use of the land and resented any federal attempts to assert control or curb their use of the public land.

Even today changes in federal policy rekindle the old public domain fights and westerners can be counted on to oppose federal control (Cawley 1993). There is a historical basis for the proprietary feelings of westerners. When the government was trying to entice people to settle the West, policies according to the Homestead Act of 1862 were aimed at disposing of land cheaply and in lots sufficiently large to support dryland farming which requires large amounts of land. Along with the homesteads came access to federal land to supplement the needs of the homesteaders' livestock. Extraction of minerals was also one of the federally sanctioned activities in the public domain. The Mining Act of 1872 made all public domain open to oil and mineral mining without payment of royalties, and it still applies today. As the title of the 1879 Commission on Public Lands indicates, there were grave abuses of the public land that forced the government to act as manager of the lands. Forests were particularly vulnerable to misuse and this misuse prompted the establishment of the National Forest system.

According to scholars of federal land policies, the major eras of federal landownership and land management were: acquisition (about 1776 to 1870), disposal (about 1790 to 1980), reservation (about 1870 to 1960), custodial management (about 1870 to 1970), intensive management (1950 to 1964), and consultation and confrontation (about 1964 to the present)(Clawson and Held 1957; Clawson 1983.) In some important ways, the Black Hills did not follow the pattern of federal management of the public domain. This study shows that the deviation from the pattern was the result of a strong commitment by people who lived on and near the Forest from about 1905 through the present to the perpetuation of the Black Hills National Forest as a multiple-use resource. The importance of the community of people who took an active management role, perhaps even a proprietary interest, in the Forest surfaced early in the life of the Black Hills National Forest and is the focus of this study. It shaped the nature of the Forest as part of the public domain.

Sustainable Use of National Forests

Sustainable use of national forests is not a new concept, in fact the national forest system was founded because of the unsustainable use of forests in the West. The conservation movement in the United States at the turn of the twentieth century had sustainable use as one of its goals (McConnell 1954.) The national forest system, established by Congress in 1891, was a product of the conservation movement. From the very beginning, national forests were multiple-use resources. Gifford Pinchot, a leader in the conservation movement and the first Chief Forester under the Department of Agriculture, stated the goal of the national forest system as *"the greatest good for the greatest number over the longest period of time"* (emphasis added) (Wilson 1905; Pinchot 1947). This statement became a slogan for the National Forests. Implicit in the statement is the notion that "conservation" did not mean preservation. The term refers to careful and controlled use, but still use. The conservation movement abhorred two kinds of waste: the senseless destruction of resources without reaping any benefit, and the failure to use resources (Pinchot 1947). The founding premise of the national forest system has remained the guiding principle for its management, although many scholars contend that the principle has long been abandoned (c.f. O'Toole 1988, 1989; Sample 1989). The Black Hills National Forest offers a valuable opportunity to study the process of managing a multiple-use resource on a sustainable basis.

Development of a sustainable scheme for managing forests is a dynamic process depending on changing resource definitions and views of forest ownership. National forests present a controlled situation for observing that process. Although all national forests have been legislatively defined as multiple-use resources, the mix of multiple uses is different in all forests because of their different physical and social environments. Additionally, both the resource definition and management possibilities are strongly influenced by local factors. Despite technical "ownership" of the national forests by the federal government, local populations have exercised ownership rights and responsibilities in various ways over time. The forest community is made up of those people in the local populations around the National Forests who have exercised these rights and responsibilities.

The basic premise guiding this research is that a national forest is used most sustainably when the forest community treats it as a multiple-use, common property resource. The conditions for sustainable use are an adoption of a multiple-use definition of the resource and active exercise of ownership rights and responsibilities by the local population.

This book covers the Black Hills National Forest (see Fig.2) from the acquisition of the area, beginning with Custer's 1874 expedition and establishment of the National Forest in 1898, through the present to see if there were periods when the forest was defined and managed as a multiple-use common property resource. How those multiple-use, common property periods differed from other periods in terms of the sustainability of use of the forest is one of the key questions.

How Can a National Forest Be a Common Property Resource?

If a pollster asked a group of people to identify who owned the National Forests, there would probably be several responses. The most popular answers would probably be the government or everyone. In this book

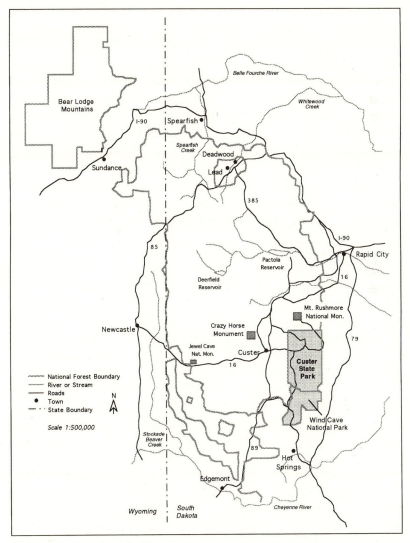

Figure 2. Map of Black Hills National Forest

you are being asked to think about ownership in a different way, as a common property resource.

Thinking about a national forest as a common property resource may seem very difficult at first. After all, the federal government holds legal title to the land; so, how can a community own something it cannot get legal title to, not to mention how can common ownership be described? The government "owns" property in different ways. For instance, a military base, or a prison, is government property to which the general public has no expectation of access. The government not only holds title to the land these institutions are on, but also controls access and makes all management decisions. National parks, on the other hand, are owned and managed by the government, but the general public has the expectation of using the parks, considering them sanctuaries of natural beauty held in trust by the government for the people. National forests fall somewhere in between no access and full access for the general public. Members of the public may use the national forests under specific conditions for private gain as well as recreation. National forests can be common property resources when the people who use and manage them are a community with a common definition of the forest. Getting past the simplistic idea that national forests are exclusively "owned" by the government is essential to studying how national forests are managed.

What Is a Common Property Resource?

Vocabulary has definitely been a stumbling block to greater understanding of common property resources. Each word in the phrase presents a problem: "common" implies everyone; "property" implies ownership that usually rests in a single entity, either public or private; and "resource" is most commonly considered in terms of economic potential of its use. None of these ordinary definitions fits the words when they are linked together in the phrase "common property resources."

Common property resources are streams of benefits flowing from a naturally occurring substance "owned" by a discrete group of people who regulate their use in a sustainable manner (McCay 1987). Ownership of a common property resource means the right to a benefit stream that is secure only as long as others respect the conditions that protect that stream (Bromley and Cernea 1989). There are three elements of a common property resource: 1. a defined resource; 2. a group of people with the recognized right to use the resource to the exclusion of others; and 3. a management plan aimed at the sustainable use of the resource in perpetuity. Parts 1 and 2 of this definition were drawn from previous common property research, most notably work by McCay and Acheson (1987), Orlove (1976), Bromley and Cernea (1989), and Ostrom (1991). The explicit reference to sustainability is not found in the earlier works, but is added here because it seems important to articulate it as a goal of common property management schemes. Perpetual existence seemed to be an assumed goal in earlier common property work.

Garrett Hardin started the modern scholarly debate on common property resources with an essay he published in *Science* in 1968 entitled "The Tragedy of the Commons." He awakened great interest in resource management with his alarming description of the economic rationality of the inevitable degradation of resources not owned by individuals or the government that would therefore lead to degradation of the whole planet.

The example Hardin used to explain the tragedy of the commons was that of a public grazing area open to all residents of a village. Each person exploited the grazing area to maximize his own profit, and in the process the grazing area was destroyed. Under Hardin's model, the finiteness of the grazing resource was known, but each person sought to maximize his own gain by burdening the resource for his own personal gain while any degradation of the resource was shared by all users (Hardin 1968). If you accept that this will happen under a common ownership scheme, then the only options are: a) privatization of the resource so the user will also bear the costs of degradation and therefore be responsible for the continued existence of the resource, or b) complete government control, where all use decisions are made by a central authority that is also responsible for preservation of the resource (Ostrom 1991). Acceptance of Hardin's tragedy of the commons reasoning resulted in discussion of only private and public options for resources such as forests. His description of a common grazing area prompted people to see the tragedy of the commons happening in many places and to many resources.

Much confusion was generated by Hardin's use of the term "commons" because what he described was actually the tragedy of "open access" resources. However, by using the word "commons," people assumed that tragedy would strike all communally held or managed resources. As studies of common property resource (CPR) management schemes have shown, tragedy is not at all inevitable with common property resources. In recognition of the scholarship that distinguished between open access and common property resources, Hardin has acknowledged that the tragedy of the commons applies to open access resources, not necessarily to common property resources (McKean and Ostrom 1995).

Acceptance of a private/public dichotomy as the only way to preserve resources has narrowed the perception of scholars looking at national forests. Researchers have focused their attention on legislative enactments and official forest service administrative policies. They have acted as if the forests are "government owned" and that the government has primary control over how the national forest is to be used (Clawson 1974; Culhane 1981; Barney 1974.) They have overlooked issues of resource definition and the role of people who live near National Forests in their management. Local influence on forest management has been well studied in developing countries, both in areas where governments do and do not "own" the forest (Poffenberger 1990).

After Hardin's 1968 article in *Science,* students of resource use, primarily economists, political scientists and anthropologists, began to examine more closely resource management schemes that were not privatized or government regulated. These scholars found that there were, in fact, common property resource (CPR) management schemes in place that were neither completely privatized nor completely government controlled. For example, Orlove (1976) studied the common property resource of grazing land in Andean mountain communities. The grazing land was a well-defined resource open to identified members of the community and a management system complete with sanctions that existed despite neither private nor government ownership. Netting (1981) described the same type of shared grazing land in the Swiss Alps. Pinkerton (1987) described how members of the salmon fishing community in British Columbia organized themselves to preserve the sustainability of the salmon supply and their access to it, to the exclusion of others, without government assistance through informal sanctions. Acheson (1988) described the way lobstermen in Maine treated the lobster as a common property resource accessible to only members of a certain community, and how they enforced their common property rights outside the limits of state law.

Although there are certain basic elements to look for in identifying common property resources, each common property scheme is unique because it depends on the way the resource is defined and the context within which it is used. Elinor Ostrom (1991) examined both successful and unsuccessful CPRs to determine what made the difference between sustainable and nonsustainable use of resources. As a result, she theorized that there was no dichotomy between private/government control and open access, but rather a continuum between private control and open access along which common property resource management schemes fall. It is her hypothesis that new institutions have developed for governing common property resources, and that in successful schemes these new institutions are blends of public and private control and are both formal and informal. While her analysis is helpful because it focuses attention on the social and economic context of the CPRs and the institutions that develop around them, the situations she analyses were relatively simple compared to a national forest. She primarily studied situations involving single-use resources and conflicts over access to the resource. This study considers a multiple-use resource that is defined and redefined continually.

The vocabulary problems associated with discussing common property resources have become clearer as CPRs are better understood. McKean and Ostrom suggest that the term "common pool resources" should be used to refer to the physical aspects of the resources, and "common property" or "common property regime" should be used to refer to the social aspects of sharing rights and duties regarding the resource (McKean and Ostrom 1995:5.) In this study, the term "common property resource" is used because it has become well known in the literature and it does not separate physical and social aspects of CPRs, instead leaving them intertwined, as they are in most situations. McKean and Ostrom also state that "common property is *shared private property* [emphasis in original] and should be considered alongside business partnerships, joint-stock corporations and partnerships" (McKean and Ostrom 1995:6). This definition seems to go back to the old private/public dichotomy that Ostrom convincingly discussed as too limiting to be useful in earlier discussions of CPRs. It also does not consider the situation of national forests, where private entities have rights to publicly owned resources. They also say that common property rights are secure if they receive appropriate legal support from governments (ibid.) This statement also seems to be a retraction of the efficacy of informal sanction power among CPR communities. Their article ends with the suggestion that bureaucratization of common property regimes for forests would be the most appropriate way to preserve common property resources. This conclusion advocates that enforcement of rights should rest with the government, not considering situations such as the national forest studied here, where the government is more of a community member than the controller when the CPR management scheme functions well.

It cannot be stressed strongly enough that common property resources exist within an integrated physical and social context. One cannot adequately study the physical resource without considering the social aspects, particularly when the discussion is over a multiple-use resource, such as a forest. Likewise the social and economic systems in the Black Hills National Forest cannot be studied without reference to the physical aspects of the forest. This book will show that dividing examination of CPRs into physical and economic components is both counterproductive and damaging to the study of multiple-use resources.

The Process of Defining a Common Property Resource

The first problem in examining a common property scheme is to identify the resource—not necessarily an easy task. Resource definition is a process, not an event (Zimmerman 1951; Rees 1990). Furthermore, it is a process within processes because it involves physical, socioeconomic, cultural, and political processes. National forests present a special opportunity for isolating the elements of the resource definition process. They are containers of resources under continual pressure from people wanting to exploit them in accordance with their own, often conflicting, definitions. Acceptable uses of national forests, established by federal legislation, are broad enough to include a wide variety of resource definitions, appropriate across the whole spectrum of different types of national forests. An operationalized definition of acceptable uses is arrived at independently in each forest. One way to tell how a resource is defined is to look at its uses. In this study, uses and attempted uses of the Black Hills National Forest defined the Forest's parameters as a multiple-use resource.

The second element of a common property resource is ownership. Ownership is resource specific and entirely different from having legal title to a piece of land over which you have a great deal of control. Ownership in this case means the right to a benefit stream that is secure only as long as others respect the conditions that protect that benefit stream (Bromley and Cernea 1989.) The critical elements are: that there is a recognizable group of people with the right to exploit the resource, and that they can exclude others. Particularly in the case of the Black Hills it is important to include cultural resources within the definition of "resource," even though one cannot put a monetary value on sacred space or the existence of wilderness in the modern world.

At first glance it might appear that national forests are owned and operated by the government, but that is not the case in reality. Ownership of national forests is a muddled concept (Blackmer 1986.) The very term "national forest" is a source of confusion in at least two respects. The common use of forest denotes trees (see Clawson 1975), but more forest elements than trees are important in national forests. Second, the term "national" modifies forests, implying some type of inclusive ownership rights for citizens at large. Citizens at large, who are so important in the definition process, do not fit neatly within traditional legal principles of private ownership (Bruce and Fortmann 1990). National forests also present a peculiar type of public ownership. They are different from both areas of exclusive government control (military bases and prisons) where the public has no expectation of use rights and areas of equal public access (national parks) where all have the same use rights. In a common property resource scheme, the right to use the resource (here, benefits of the forest) is synonymous with membership in the resource community. The ownership question is answered by examining who successfully or unsuccessfully attempted to use the Black Hills National Forest. Political economists, presently in the forefront of common property resource research use the term "social capital" to refer to the community with the strong sense of identification and responsibility on the part of members of the community (Ostrom 1992.) By using social capital instead of community, the users become quantifiable and objective. Social capital a is network of social relationships that can be counted on to govern use of the resource. It is a term that comes from economics and allows a severance between the physical and social/economic aspects of the CPR. This researcher does not find the term "social capital" helpful and will continue to use the term "community." The trend in the discipline of geography is to examine the human dimensions of physical change, reuniting physical and social processes, not separating them.

The third element, a management scheme based on sustainability, is extremely important with respect to environmental conservation on local and global levels. Each common property resource has a recognized management scheme attached to it that is adhered to by members of the ownership group and has the goal of sustainable use of the resource for the foreseeable future. The management scheme includes formal or informal enforcement mechanisms (see, for example Acheson 1988.) The collective management scheme is a crucial element of the common property resource concept.

The ownership and management elements are intertwined, because management is certainly an aspect of ownership responsibility. Previous scholarly investigation of national forests has centered on their management by the government, as if the government were solely in control of forest management. Many studies have focused on the public policy and economic efficiency of forest management (Sedjo 1983; Krutilla, Bowes and Wilman 1983; Repetto and Holmes 1983; O'Toole 1988). However, they have treated the public as consumers of forest resources, not as definers of the forest and they have treated the Forest Service as the controlling party on forest use. Consequently, both the definition of the national forest as a resource and the true nature of the management scheme have not been closely scrutinized.

National forests include both technically public and legally private lands when they are surrounded by a National Forest. Notwithstanding those formal types of ownership, there is a different form of ownership operating in this arena: that of common property ownership. The idea of conceptualizing U. S. national forests as common property resources has not been seriously pursued because of a lack of understanding of CPRs. Deacon and Johnson (1985) state that there is a parallel between publicly held assets and CPRs, but they have confused CPRs with open access resources in much the same way that Garrett Hardin did in his tragedy of the commons theory. They erroneously characterize CPR management as the absence of well-defined rights and rewards for proper management (Deacon and Johnson at 4). In the book, *Whose Trees,* Fortmann and Bruce (1990) have collected studies of land tenure and tree tenure from around the world. The authors of the individual studies exhibit a clear understanding of common property rights concerning forests. However, in the introduction, Bruce and Fortmann fail to apply such an understanding to U.S. national forests. They say,

> a sort of customary law has grown up around the use of national forest land in which proximity gives rights. Local residents consider the national forest 'theirs'. This sometimes unarticulated customary practice stands at odds in a number of ways with national statutory law that assigns rights in the forest to all citizens. (Bruce and Fortmann at 6)

The problem with that characterization is that national forest use, governed by statutes and regulations, vests not in all citizens but in those whose intended use falls within the sanctioned uses. By failing to examine the composition of the user group and the range of acceptable uses, Fortmann and Bruce missed an opportunity to clarify use patterns in national forests.

It has been a great mistake to characterize efficient resource use as either private or government controlled. As Ostrom (1991) has shown, some of the most successful common property resource schemes are governed by institutions that are a mix of public and private entities. That was indeed the case in the Black Hills during its most sustainable use periods.

At different periods in its history, the Black Hills National Forest has been a common property resource and during those times the management plan has been geared toward sustainable management of the national forest as a multiple-use resource. Because the definition of the national forest is a dynamic process, both actual and potential forest users have had much to say about that definition. There were two common property resource periods in the history of the Black Hills National Forest. These two periods were not the same; they developed under different conditions and with different resource definitions, but both contained the elements of a common property management scheme.

The Black Hills

The Black Hills are a very special place to a wide variety of people. Travelers across the Great Plains, now and in the past, can see them rising above the plains long before they reach them. From a distance, they appear black, because pines are the predominant vegetation. Figure 3a shows a view of the northern Hills and Figure 3b shows a view of the Southern Hills. Over the years there have been suggestions that their name be changed to Black Mountains because the tallest peak, Harney Peak, in the southern Hills is 7,242 feet, although the elevations of the surrounding plains are from 3,000 to 3500 feet (Froiland 1990:11). The change is usually advocated by promoters of tourism. By the standards of the Rocky Mountains, "hills" seems like an appropriate term, and the term has stuck.

The name "Black Hills" is taken from the name "*Paha Sapa*" in the Sioux language, which translates as Black Hills. The Oglala Sioux Indians usually camped within sight of the Black Hills, and considered them a sacred place, also naming them *Wamakaognake E'Cante,* "the Heart of Everything That Is" (Fools Crow 1987). Chapter 2 contains more about the Sioux definition of the Hills as a cultural resource, although Lazarus (1990) provides a much more comprehensive study of the ongoing Sioux legal claim.

As Fig. 2 shows, the Black Hills contain Mount Rushmore, the Shrine of Democracy, visited by millions of people each year. Sturgis,

Figure 3a. Photograph of Northern Black Hills

Figure 3b. Photograph of Southern Black Hills

S.D., one of the towns in the Black Hills, also hosts a yearly motorcycle rally when bikers enjoy the scenic beauty of the area. Being centrally located within the continental United States, there are also a number of defense establishments in the area, including Ellsworth Air Force Base and missile storage sites. The chambers of commerce of the Black Hills towns once tried to have both the United Nations and the second capitol of the United States located in Rapid City, S.D., "the Gateway City to the Hills" (RCJ 1 March 1950:4).

Besides the beauty of this distinctive geographic feature in western South Dakota and eastern Wyoming, the Hills also contain much of the mineral wealth of South Dakota. The abundance of gold had an extremely strong influence on modern development of western South Dakota. The influence is not as great in Wyoming because most of the Black Hills and their minerals are on the South Dakota side of the border. Seven counties contain parts of the Black Hills: Crook and Weston counties in Wyoming and Custer, Fall River, Lawrence, Meade and Pennington Counties in South Dakota. (See Fig 3c.) All of these counties contain both agricultural land and forested land. Most of the forested land is in either the Black Hills National Forest or Custer State Park.

Why Study the Black Hills National Forest?

The Black Hills National Forest (BHNF) offered several unique opportunities for the study of the multiple use resource definition process. BHNF was one of the first national forests established in 1898. Settlement of the Black Hills had really begun in 1876 with the gold rush, first to the southern end of the Hills (see Fig. 3b), and then to the richer northern area of the Hills (see Fig.3a). The frontier towns that were built were established immediately after a gold strike and abandoned just as quickly when the vein gave out. This settlement pattern meant that there were small towns throughout the Hills and larger towns near profitable gold deposits. Although the first gold was found near the town of Custer, S.D. in the south, the richest deposits were found in Lead, S.D. and Deadwood, S.D. in the north. Custer, however, was not completely abandoned after the gold deposits proved to be unprofitable, and remained a population center in the south, serving mostly as an agricultural center. Deadwood and Lead dominated the area in population and wealth, and Rapid City, S.D. outside the Hills, served as a gateway, but was not one of the earliest settlements. So, unlike many national forests, the Black Hills National Forest was established within the context of

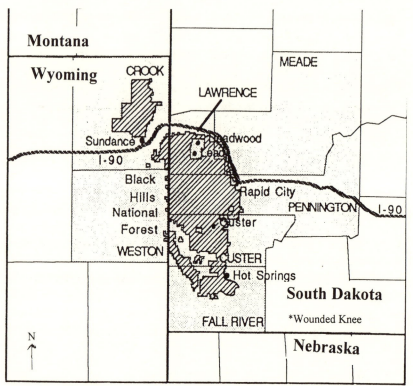

Scale- 1" = 105 miles

Figure 3c. Black Hills Counties

settled towns. Other national forests are located in remote areas, but development of the Black Hills preceded establishment of the BHNF.

The BHNF was also a model forest after the Department of Agriculture (USDA) became responsible for National Forests in 1905. Gifford Pinchot, the first Chief Forester in the USDA, treated the BHNF as the flagship forest for the nation, implementing multiple-use principles and trying out multiple-use management models there first (Pinchot 1947).

The BHNF and the total Black Hills area have not only great economic significance, but also great cultural significance. This juxtaposition of economics and culture puts both the definition of resource and the definition of multiple use at issue. Because of the long, uninterrupted history of multiple use, the BHNF was chosen as a place to study the process of defining and implementing multiple-use principles.

The Black Hills National Forest has well-defined boundaries that coincide with the outlines of forest vegetation to a considerable extent. (See Figure 2.) The name "Black Hills National Forest" will be used throughout this study even though it was administratively separated into the Black Hills National Forest (northern part) and the Harney National Forest (southern part) from 1910 to 1954. Both forests were managed in similar fashions when they were separate, and the split and later joined was a matter of administrative convenience and budget concerns. BHNF has also been a stable forest in the sense that its boundaries have been relatively stable and there have not been sudden and disruptive changes in management policy. The Black Hills National Forest is conspicuous by its absence among descriptions of poorly managed forests.

The exact definition of the BHNF forest community is basic to the question of who "owns" the Forest and is what this book is about. The community is not officially defined anywhere and the reader should feel free to decide whether or not to agree with the my conclusions.

As a point of beginning, the National Forest Management Act of 1976 requires that forest plans for each National Forest include a definition of the "Human Resource Unit," which represents the geographic area with the best access and most direct interest in the particular national forest. In the BHNF forest plan, the seven counties containing the BHNF are the Human Resource Unit. This includes Crook and Weston counties in Wyoming and Custer, Fall River, Lawrence, Meade, and Pennington in South Dakota. Designating the local study area as the seven counties containing the BHNF excludes the Sioux Nation because the Sioux Nation is not a part of any South Dakota county. The BHNF is completely outside the Reservations where the members of the Sioux Indian Nation live. To a certain degree this reflects the political and social reality of the area; the Sioux Nation's claim to the Black Hills is still outstanding, although most non-Indian South Dakotans take either 1876 (the date of the Manypenny Commission) or 1877 (when Congress unilaterally declared that the Black Hills belonged to the United States) as the termination of Sioux ownership of the Black Hills (Lazarus 1990). This is not to say that the Sioux have had no influence in defining the Black Hills National Forest, but only to say that their influence has been from the outside, and often adversarial.

Most of the focus will be on South Dakota's part of the BHNF. The Wyoming sections are so small and represent such a small proportion of the national forest lands within Wyoming that after initial investigation it served no purpose to study the BHNF in relation to Wyoming. On the other hand, the Black Hills are of great importance to South Dakota. They have been a strong part of South Dakota's economy since prestatehood days.

The BHNF is also influenced by national trends, represented by Forest Service policy, congressional legislation and presidential directives on the one hand and nationally based environmental groups on the other. Not all national environmental legislation or activity impacts on the Black Hills and only that having at least a marginal impact will be discussed.

How Does One Demonstrate Ownership of a U.S. National Forest as a Common Property Resource?

This is a question that has not been asked before, so answering it is a challenge. As discussed earlier ownership of a national forest is more informal than formal when one considers the requirements for a common property regime, but there are clear requirements to establish that a common property resource exists which guided the research. The three basic questions are: How is the resource defined? Who exercises ownership rights over it? Is there a sustainable management plan? Answering these questions required an extensive understanding of human and physical context of the Black Hills area as it related to the Black Hills National Forest. The essence of the study was to examine the relationships surrounding the Black Hills National Forest over the years and to identify significant patterns relating to resource definition and sustainable use. Fortunately there are several models of studies in areas other than common property resources that when combined were helpful in both identifying what information to look for and how to analyze it.

Cole Harris, a historical geographer, has discussed the problem of how to discover the past roots of a place from the vantage point of the present (1978:123). He says that the researcher must develop a historic mind, which really requires her to immerse herself as much as possible in the various historic contexts that she is studying. Harris recognized that many of the tools available to people studying the present are not available to people studying the past because of the limited life spans of informants, and loss or lack of records. Therefore, he says that the researcher has to look at everything available that might even be tangentially related to the subject of research. Isolated facts may take on meaning when put in context. The technique that Harris calls the historic mind requires the researcher to make judgments about the information uncovered and come to supportable conclusions. Understanding the context is the most important factor for Harris. Context includes both human and physical systems. Using Harris' technique of the historical, the elements of a common property resource guided examination of the context of the Black Hills National Forest.

There was a wealth of information about the Black Hills and the BHNF, but it came from a wide variety of sources. Relevant information included anything pertaining to South Dakota or eastern Wyoming, and about the subjects of national forests; forests in general; the Black Hills; the Black Hills National Forest; mining; timber; lumber; recreation; tourism; grazing; stock raising; agriculture; water use or availability; population gain, loss or composition; migration; census; economic climate; Sioux Indian claims; federal spending; economic development plans; or scientific research on the Black Hills. The bibliography contains a list of the materials consulted to construct the history of the resource definition of the Black Hills National Forest.

Another factor that needs to be considered is that research such as this has an experiential component. Experience is relevant in two ways. First, the researcher experiences the region during fieldwork and forms independent opinions about the area. Second, historical and contemporary accounts of the Black Hills are really the product of the experiences of the people who wrote them. It is important to note their experiential nature because accounts may differ considerably, and it is part of the researcher's task to reconstruct the context of the accounts (Relph 1981). This was particularly important in dealing with the *Rapid City Journal* as an information source. The *Rapid City Journal* was published from 1878 through the present and provided a wealth of information. It was important to put the role of the newspaper into perspective. The *Rapid City Journal* (hereafter RCJ) turned out to be the primary source of data about the local and regional contexts and the perceptions of the BHNF as a resource. It was not until 1897 when the Black Hills Forest Reserve was set aside that there was any newspaper space devoted to the forest, and there was not much in the way of journalism until after the turn of the century. The types of information found in the newspaper were the rules governing use of the BHNF; reports of use of the forest; stories about use of the forest by area residents; stories about conflicts over use, misuse, and development plans; and editorials and letters to the editor. In most years revenue statistics on the national forest were reported in the local paper, giving board feet of timber cut, fence posts, etc. and the amount of money that went back to the counties. In addition, stories about the local economy, tourism promotion, and mineral industries helped fill in the socioeconomic context. Early in the study period, when it started to publish more than just land claims, the paper took on a booster role for the area. It had a standard story about the natural history and contemporary climate that was included each week. The RCJ published estimates of the population between censuses, which always turned out to be too high, but were extremely valuable in obtaining federal money for post offices, roads, and public buildings. Until the mid-1960s, there was little news of controversies over the Forest, but when the forest was becoming degraded, the paper reported often on local efforts to change management strategies. With regard to Indian relations, the RCJ reported from the Euro-American point of view and reported mostly on the efforts of the Sioux to regain the Black Hills. However, they also did stories on how the Sioux Indians believed that the Black Hills were sacred, and published Dee Brown's book, *Bury My Heart at Wounded Knee,* as a series. During the second Wounded Knee confrontation in 1973, (the first was in 1890), the newspaper became clearly an advocate for the white community and the Indians would not speak to RCJ reporters. When the first National Forest Management Plan was being prepared in 1982 and 1983, the newspaper actively publicized meetings, the details of the plan, and controversies about management of the Forest. The newspaper was a source of context, but it was also published in a context. Newspapers often have points of view and they need to be checked against other information on the area (Franzosi 1987). The lack of a newspaper report does not mean that an event did not occur (Danzger 1975). The experiential or phenomenological aspects of the newspaper were considered.

The Black Hills have a wealth of information on many aspects of their history. The expected primary source of data on the National Forest itself was the Supervisor's Office of the Black Hills National Forest in Custer. It was hoped that historical records would be available from the time of the establishment of the Forest, but this was not the case. Records are required to be kept for only ten years and many records no longer exist. However, there is a historical records file at the Supervisor's office, that contains extensive records back to the beginning of the BHNF, but there has not been any regular procedure for adding records to the historical file. The main criterion seems to have been that someone in the Forest Service thought the records were important. The people who worked in the National Forest seemed to value historical information and the historical role of the Black Hills National Forest. Therefore, the historical files provided a valuable resource, but they do not contain a complete history of the Forest. They contain correspondence and background information on some Forest Service policies and some disputes over use of Forest land. They also provide valuable insight into the decision-making process within the Forest Service and how the Forest Service viewed the community at various times. There is no reason to believe that even those controversies reflected in the historic files are reported in full. The presence of information in the historic files is not taken as an indication that the Forest Service officially thought the recorded matters had any more significance than matters which were not recorded.

In addition to the historic files in the Forest Supervisor's Office, a search was conducted of government documents pertaining to the Black Hills National Forest (including the former Harney National Forest). This search yielded management plans, reports, and evaluations. U.S. Department of Agriculture statistics on national forests from 1905 forward were sometimes helpful. Information on animal grazing, timber harvest, and recreational use of the national forests was regularly reported. However, after the early 1950s statistics were reported by state, not by national forest. South Dakota and Wyoming each contain more than one national forest.

Towns have not only kept records since they were founded, but histories have been written. The Black Hills were clearly part of the excitement of settling the frontier, and there are many accounts of it. Initially, it was thought that population dynamics had a strong, independent influence on sustainable use, but that was not the case. One early research hypothesis concluded that definitional changes of the national forest were the product of migration to the area by people with different views of the forest and natural resources; and another stated that definitional changes were the result of population growth. After extensive review of population data from state censuses (taken at the midpoint between the federal decennial censuses), federal censuses, and vital statistics, it was concluded that population dynamics were not an important factor in the resource definition process. Times when forest resources were being overtaxed had more to do with the deer census than the human population census.

Part of developing a historic mind about the BHNF was to do more than report on facts. In order to understand the facts, they had to be looked at in many ways. Understanding of the meaning of the Black Hills National Forest to those who lived there (Relph 1981; Lowenthal 1976) required looking at it from their point of view. The forest landscape also had social meaning that was evident from spatial patterns of use and claims of ownership (Jackson 1984; Meinig 1979; Duncan and Duncan 1988; Cosgrove 1984; and Ley 1977). The spatial patterns of use were particularly evident in the Black Hills National Forest because agricultural land is hard to come by in that area; and all agricultural land was excluded from the forest and privately owned. Therefore, the forest lines usually follow the tree lines. BHNF contains places of cultural symbolism (Rowntree and Conkey 1980) such as Mount Rushmore and culturally defined sacred space (Tuan 1978) claimed by the Sioux Indian Nation. Questions of resource use and management could best be explored with reference to their entire context, physical as well as human (White 1986; Blaikie and Brookfield 1987; Hecht 1988; Bennett 1969; and Hudson, 1983).

Putting together the story of the Black Hills National Forest required analyzing the information within a format that would take into consideration complex human and physical systems which changed over time. In the BHNF the actions of individuals, interest groups, and government entities all interacted with each other and the physical environment. There were different levels of interaction and different results of interaction. By using Anthony Giddens' (1984) concept of structuration it was possible to put the pieces of the puzzle together. Social theorists have always argued over whether agents (individuals) or social structures control action and social change. Giddens says that instead of attributing change to either agents or structures, one should look at social change as a recursive relationship between agents and structures. The relationship is recursive because agents modify social structures and social structures modify agents at the same time, making change a mixture agency and structure. Giddens also divided resources into two categories: allocative resources that include material objects, natural resources, or money; and authoritative resources that include the power to distribute the allocative resources. He also says that humans act on three different levels of consciousness: unconscious, practical consciousness (doing things by routine), and discursive consciousness. Giddens provides the outline for analysis, although physical processes are much more important in tracing the history of the BHNF than in the usual sociological situations where structuration is used. Through the geographic concept of political ecology, structuration is readily applicable to the BHNF (Zimmerer 1991:444).

Structuration helps organize the story of the BHNF by allowing us to sort out how individuals (for example, homesteaders and miners) changed and were changed by structures such as the Forest Service. Socially organized groups, such as the Izaak Walton League, altered the way other groups, perhaps the chambers of commerce, acted as their own actions were being altered. There were clearly allocative resources within the Black Hills National Forest that were constantly being defined and redefined. The authoritative resources governing the allocative resources also changed, which enables the reader to see how the BHNF could be a common property resource during some periods and not during others. The actions of the Forest Service were not automatically authoritative. The forest community changed in composition over time, but also possessed and exercised varying levels of authority. Even the levels of consciousness are relevant to this story because some actions, of both groups and individuals, seemed unconscious (or without thought of the consequences), such as stripping the Hills of trees for mining before the National Forest was born; some had a practical (routine) consciousness about them, such as dumping waste into streams; and others were the product of discursive consciousness, such as whether to create lakes, or build Mount Rushmore or Crazy Horse.

The story of the BHNF is a complex one. It is different from the stories of other national forests, and yet there are probably similarities as well. This is not just the story of the BHNF, but more importantly it is the story of the process of resource definition over time and the formation and reformation of the forest community and its changing relationship to the Forest Service. Changing environmental attitudes are reflected in the resource definition changes, but they are local changes, not merely reflections of national changes.

Structure of the Book

The chapters are centered on different resource definition periods. Each chapter describes the context for the resource definition, the consequences of the resource definition, and whether the BHNF was a common property resource during the particular resource definition period.

In chapter 2, two different periods are described: 1874 to 1897, the open access gold mine period, and 1898 to 1904, when the government tried to establish control over the Forest as government property. The open-access gold mine period began with discovery of gold in 1874 and includes removal of the Black Hills from the control of the Sioux Indian Nation. It was a period of rapid development in the Hills as miners and prospectors scoured the Hills for gold. It ended with the Deadwood/Lead area dominating the economy of the Black Hills. This period also was the catalyst for setting aside a National Forest because timber was viewed only as an adjunct to mining and whole hillsides were stripped. In the second period, 1898 to 1904, the Black Hills National Forest was established, at least in name and on the map, but the Department of the Interior had great difficulty gaining control. Miners and homesteaders had not been in favor of the national forest and were not inclined to alter their behavior. The Department of the Interior did not have the resources to firmly regulate the activities in the entire forest, or even to provide fire protection. This was not a common property resource period because there was no shared definition of the resource, forest community, or sustainable management plan.

The first common property resource period (1905 to 1919) is discussed in chapter 3. When responsibility for the National Forests was transferred to U.S. Department of Agriculture in 1905, Gifford Pinchot became the first Chief Forester. He had been trained in the European tradition of multiple-use forests and put that plan to work in the United States. Pinchot chose the Black Hills National Forest as his model forest where he tried out new ideas before recommending them for use in other forests. One of his biggest contributions was to essentially foster a forest community and treat the BHNF as a common property resource. He insisted on having local people working for the Forest Service and called on all who lived within the forest bounds to become managers of the forest. He encouraged homesteading on the agricultural land to fully use the land around the National Forest as well as the forest itself. Most people living on or near the forest at that time were multiple users both individually and as a group. The uses included timber for building houses, and as a money crop, fence posts, and the land was also used for mining, and grazing.

Chapter 4 covers a long period of time, from 1919 to the mid-1960s. It starts with the demise of the first common property scheme during World War I as the population of the Black Hills dropped when people either went to war or to work in the wartime industries. During this time the Forest Service tried to more actively and closely manage the forest as it had from 1898 to 1904. There were several management schemes that helped destroy the common property definition. One was zoning of the forest, which involved having separate zones set aside for certain uses, such as a timber area, a grazing area, and a recreation area instead of mixed usage. Working circles were also introduced as a way to focus the timber industry on established towns and mills to promote economic development. This period includes the carving of Mount Rushmore and the initiation of the Crazy Horse monument, showing conflict between groups demonstrated by landscape symbols. During the New Deal, the BHNF benefited greatly from infrastructure projects that changed the nature of the Hills substantially. There are no natural lakes in the Black Hills, but the New Deal and the Civilian Conservation Corps added lakes that became the core of the recreation industry. Scenic highways were constructed and local access increased. There was a spirit of entrepreneurship that pervaded the later parts of the period from the late 1940s to the mid-1960s. Multiple uses clashed, and no one seemed to have a sense of the forest as a whole being a multiple-use resource. The watershed was the part of the forest that showed signs of distress, indicating that the forest was no longer thought of as a multiple-use resource, but rather as a many-use resource.

Chapter 5 discusses the unfolding of a second common property period from the mid-1960s to 1971 when local people tried to exert control in response to degradation of the forest in the prior periods. People no longer left management up to the Forest Service. They questioned policies and made a fuss over misuse. Mining practices were fingered as environmental problems. Groups began to organize around issues. The lack of cohesion on a definition of a multiple-use resource and the infancy of any forest community really prevent this from being a common property period.

Chapter 6 covers 1972 to 1994, when a common property community was beginning to take management responsibility for the BHNF. Although this last period approaches a common property management scheme, there are some serious shortfalls. The Forest Service was required by the National Forest Management Act of 1976 to prepare a forest plan for each National Forest and the preparation of the plans included public input. This requirement may have overstated the expectations of the Forest Service for the involvement of local people in management, but there was movement toward agreement on the definition of a multiple-use resource. The period falls short of a common property period because there is not any agreement by all users to also be managers. Recreational uses (primarily reservoir uses)require great amounts of management and service, but take no responsibility for sharing the cost. During this period there was also conflict over Sioux Indian exclusion from the forest community. Wilderness areas became a demand that ended up in litigation, something that would not happen in an ideal common property regime. This last period could have gone either way on the common property issue, but it is leaning toward government control with a bureaucratic framework.

The Black Hills National Forest has changed considerably since 1898. Resource categories have been added, procedures have been bureaucratized, but the fundamental question will always remain—How is the Black Hills National Forest defined as a resource and who exercises control and management of it.

Chapter 2

The Early Years in the Black Hills

The Black Hills are the "easternmost extension of the Rocky Mountains" covering about six thousand square miles, "extending approximately 120 miles in a north-south direction and approximately 40–50 miles in an east-west direction" (Froiland 1990:11). They form an elliptical outcropping in the High Plains, and their forest vegetation is very distinct from the grasslands that surround them. Streams and rivers flow from the Black Hills in an easterly direction to the Missouri River. Long before the white explorers made forays into the Hills, Plains Indian Nations claimed ownership rights.

By the time white men started exploring the Black Hills, the Lakota people, members of the Sioux Indian Nation, having been driven west from Minnesota by white settlement, had claimed them. In the process, the Sioux drove both the Arikara and Cheyenne Nations from that territory (Milton 1977:41). There was no written history of the Sioux Nation's use of the Black Hills contemporary with their occupation, but their myths and oral history allow a glimpse of what it may have been like. Because the Sioux Nation is still a vital nation, what has been written in the present gives us something by which we can understand their past, although their intervening history colors both past memories and present descriptions. The Black Hills were, and are, considered sacred by the Sioux Indians. They communicated that belief to whites who came in contact with them. They had several names for the Black Hills including the one adopted by the whites, *Paha Sapa,* translated as Black Hills; they also called them *Wamakaognaka E'Cante* meaning the "Heart of Everything That Is" and *O'onakezin,* Place of Shelter (Fools Crow, 1987).

29

The Sioux were a Plains tribe and did not establish permanent settlements similar to the Euro-American settlements of the first explorers.
They did not dwell within the forest except when they needed shelter.
They believed and still believe, that the Great Spirit dwelled in the
Black Hills. Some places, such as the warm mineral springs in what is
now Hot Springs, S. D., had particular significance because of their cu-
rative powers. One legend tells of how Indians came from all over North
America to be healed at *Minnekahta* (or "warm springs") when an epi-
demic struck all tribes before the time of the European contact (Clark
1927). Another legend says that "the dark of night turns the rocks into
spirits that sing strange songs awakening the echoes. From holes in rock
walls healing waters flow and the people fill their buffalo-horn cups
with clear water and drink it to become pure. From the great needles of
rock that touch the sky the medicine men call the Mighty Spirit" (Workers of the South Dakota Writers' Project, Works Progress Administration, 1988 4th printing).

Another Lakota myth tells how the Black Hills were created. There
was an empty prairie where many creatures roamed and killed each
other and were killed by humans. Humans desired order so they held a
race among all creatures to establish order. They built a very large circular racetrack and all of the beings took part in the race that lasted several days. The track sank under the weight of the racers, and as it sank
a mound appeared in the middle that burst open, killing the animals with
lava and leaving the spectacular rock formation known as *Paha Sapa*
(LaPointe 1976). Black Elk, a famous medicine man told a different
story of the racetrack. In his story, the Black Hills already existed, and
it was a race between two-legged creatures and four-legged creatures to
see if humans or animals would have supremacy. The race was run on
the red racetrack that encircles the Black Hills, and the humans won.
The prize was the bow and arrow and the land where the race was held
which was their promised land (Rezatto 1989; DeMallie 1984). This
myth predates the Lakota occupation of the Hills but gave the Lakota
reason for seizing the area from other Indian Nations around 1776
(Froiland 1990).

There are elements of all these myths present in the modern day
Black Hills. The Needles, an ancient granite formation resembling needles standing on end, is still a major attraction for people visiting the
Hills. The Black Hills are surrounded by a red-colored soil "track." The
mineral waters of Hot Springs have been used by Euro-Americans as
well as Indians for medicinal purposes. The night noises in the Hills are

very different than the night noises of the prairie, and their sounds can be intimidating.

The Sioux people did not leave obvious evidence of their occupation of the Hills, because they considered them sacred. They went into the Hills for lodgepoles and to hunt. They lived on the Plains. Information about the Sioux heritage is provided not just because they have still not settled their claim to the Black Hills, but because their use of the Hills had a strong influence on the way the Hills were used after the Indians were confined to reservations.

The Discovery of a Potential Resource by Euro-Americans

The Black Hills' first explorations by Euro-Americans has interested historians for some time. A summary of that history is provided here because it forms the initial context for changing the resource definition of the Black Hills from sacred territory to economic resource.

The Black Hills were part of the Louisiana Purchase in 1803 (Milton 1977). As was true for most of the Louisiana Purchase, the U.S. Government did not know much about the area. President Thomas Jefferson commissioned Captains Lewis and Clark to explore the area and report on every aspect of what they learned about the land, rivers, minerals, and people inhabiting the area. The president basically wanted a report on everything and everyone they encountered (ibid). Lewis and Clark did not explore the Black Hills during their expedition from 1804 to 1806, however they did meet French traders who had been trapping in the Black Hills whom they invited to join their expedition. The sketchy description of the Hills (which they called the Black Mountains) provided by the traders, Jean Valle and Baptiste LePage, was included in Lewis and Clark's report (Froiland 1990). Several other hunting expeditions came within sight of the Hills, but they were not entered until 1823 when Jedediah Smith led a group of mountainmen into the Southern Hills through Buffalo Gap (ibid.). Neither of those descriptions contained any information that suggested that the Black Hills would be of great value to the U.S. government, although this was a time of great expansion when all land between the Atlantic and Pacific Oceans was being incorporated into the United States. Congress was busily passing legislation during this time period to encourage people to move West and to protect them when they made their journey across the Indian lands. Although the lands had been set aside by Congress, they blocked some of the best routes West.

At this time the West was seen as a vast storehouse of potential wealth (Young, RCJ 28 August 1885:35), and the goal was to reach it, by bypassing the Indian lands which looked unproductive. There is reliable evidence that Father DeSmet, a missionary priest serving the Indians in the Dakotas, had heard of gold in the Black Hills by 1834, but kept the information secret because of his fear for the integrity of Indian Territory (Parker 1966:12). Under the Treaty of Fort Laramie in 1851, Sioux lands were designated to clearly include the Black Hills. Of particular importance to the Black Hills was the provision that gave settlers and miners safe passage along the Platte River. While the Platte River does not even abut the Black Hills, it was a clear sign that "white men" would be coming and Sioux land was threatened. It was also a clear sign that if Indian lands stood between gold and the settled East, Indian lands would be crossed regardless of the treaties. Colonel William Harney, who is of later importance regarding the Black Hills, enforced the Fort Laramie Treaty by attacking Little Thunder's camp after some travelers had been harassed. "With 1,300 troops well armed against a few hundred Sioux, many of them women and children, the encounter was a massacre" (Lazarus 1991:23).

The Treaty of 1868 between the United States and the Sioux also left the Black Hills in Sioux hands, but rumors were starting that there might be gold in the Black Hills. Prospectors for gold and settlers looking for good land did not respect the treaty provisions that were supposed to keep them off Indian land. To satisfy their constituents, Congress authorized other trails through Indian territory without asking the Indians for permission (Froiland 1990:70). Private expeditions entered the Hills after the Fort Laramie Treaty of 1851. The Treaty of 1868 did not satisfy the speculators because it did not allow them into the Hills legally. They had been to the Hills and seen gold by the time that treaty was negotiated and demanded U.S. government protection of their safety while they were illegally in the Hills. Instead of settling disagreements, the Treaty of 1868 made things worse because it reaffirmed Sioux ownership of the Hills and the Indians felt more justified in attacking illegal settlers. Under the Treaty of 1868 territory west of the Missouri River and east of the Powder River, including the Black Hills, was ceded to the Sioux Indians. In this treaty the signatory tribes agreed to live on this reservation and the U.S. government pledged to keep whites off it. The nature of the Indian claims is not the main subject of this study but will be a factor in the resource definition process. Because the flood of prospectors and settlers could not be abated by the U.S. government, the only solution was to buy the Black Hills, a solution that to this day has proven to be impossible (Parker 1966; Lazarus 1990).

This study of change in the resource definition process in the Black Hills and subsequently in the Black Hills National Forest really begins with the U.S. government's official expedition into the region in 1874. In 1874 General George Armstrong Custer was commissioned to explore the Black Hills for places to build outposts that would ensure the safety of people moving West. His expeditionary force included geologists, prospectors, photographers, and journalists. General Custer officially began the resource redefinition process when he reported finding gold in the Black Hills. Custer's explorations were primarily confined to the southern Black Hills where the present Custer County is located. His entourage was meticulous in describing what they found, even photographing much of the landscape. Custer did find gold throughout the valleys, not nuggets but enough to reward a man for his labor (Newton and Jenney 1880:16, quoting Custer's report). Knowing now that the gold in the Black Hills was predominantly in the Northern Hills, it seems likely that reports of gold distributed throughout the Hills were based on earlier private expeditions and were attributed to Custer, magnified by the miners and prospectors who accompanied him, and were further embellished by the Eastern press (Newton and Jenney 1880:16).

There was another kind of gold found too, the agricultural suitability of the land, particularly good grazing land. The Hills had plenty of deer, elk, bear, and mountain goats, and the Plains supported large herds of buffalo. There were enough streams with water, even in the summer, so it was clear that agriculture could be supported. The combination of the mineral gold and good agricultural potential was touted as "gold above and below the ground" (Dodge 1876).

Newton and Jenney, scientists commissioned by the government to explore the area in 1875, described the Great Sioux Reservation as follows:

> This large reservation, excepting the Black Hills, their immediate vicinity, and the narrow valleys of some of the more important streams, is a most inhospitable region, desolate and barren, and includes a large area of the well-known sterile and clayey tracts of "badlands". . . . It may be said with truth that the Black Hills include all the desirable land in the reservation and all the useful timber, and by those who view the treatment and future of the Indians in this region in a purely humanitarian spirit the presence of gold in the Black Hills has been regarded as unfortunate, for if it were not for its discovery, this beautifully timbered and grassed region would afford them an excellent retreat during their initiation into the simpler labors of civilization. (Newton and Jenney 1880:5)

Probably the most important part of the report of the exploration of the Black Hills by scientists accompanying General Custer in 1874 was the notation that the Sioux considered them sacred, but they *were not using them* (emphasis added) (Newton and Jenney 1880). The cultural uses of the Black Hills as the home of spirits, a place that yielded necessities, where the Sioux went for spiritual renewal and tribal rites had no meaning to the Euro-American culture when compared with the possible economic uses of the Hills.

Creation of an Open-Access Gold Mine — 1875 to 1897

It is difficult to date precisely when the Black Hills became an open-access gold mine, but the process started between 1855 and 1874. Watson Parker (1966) dates the beginning of the gold rush itself from the 1874 entry of the private Gordon Party that followed General Custer into the Hills and set up a stockade in which they lived during the winter of 1874 to 1875. Although they were removed by the army in 1875, their reports of gold could not be squelched. After reports of gold became public, the prospectors came in droves in 1875 even though white entry into the Hills was a breach of the Treaty of 1868. The migrant miners put great pressure on the U. S. government to obtain jurisdiction over the Black Hills (Newton and Jenney 18). Although the military escorted many groups of miners out of the Hills, both the military and the prospectors regarded the evictions as temporary. The military even allowed the illegal migrants to plat the town of Custer to preserve their land claims and the structure of the town for their inevitable return. Mining claims were protected when miners cooperated by leaving when the military asked them to.

As the military removed the miners and intercepted groups of settlers, the government, through the Allison Commission, negotiated with the Sioux for the sale of the Black Hills. Negotiations failed and the Sioux Nation and the United States went to war. The Sioux defeated General Custer and the Seventh Cavalry at Little Big Horn in 1876, and news of that outcome reached Washington, D.C., in the middle of the centennial celebrations (Lazarus 1991). The timing of the announcement fanned the flames of anger and made the United States all the more determined to take the Hills. The Sioux had won the Battle of Little Bighorn, but ultimately lost the war and treaty negotiations began again for the purpose of selling the Black Hills to the United States. In 1876 the Manypenny Commission gave the Sioux the choice of ceding the Hills or starving, a threat which was extremely likely to be carried out because the Sioux were on reservations by then. Even under the terms of the Manypenny agreement, three-fourths of the Indian males had to ratify the sale of the Hills and all concede that this ratification provision was not met. By the congressional act of February 28, 1877, Congress unilaterally imposed the Manypenny Agreement and claimed ownership of the Black Hills (Lazarus 1991). Figure 4 shows the outlines of the Sioux Reservation after Congress excised the Black Hills from the Reservation in 1877.

Even before congressional imposition of the Manypenny terms, the Black Hills were well populated by whites. The towns of Deadwood and Hill City had been incorporated in 1876 (Bullock 1962; Wedge 1979). In describing the counties of Custer (including present day Fall River County), Lawrence (including present day Meade County) and Pennington Counties, the 1880 federal census for Dakota Territory listed 1875 as their formation date, but 1877 as their official organization date. No one even tried to disguise the presence of settlers prior to Congress' action to take the Hills from the Sioux. According to Newton and Jenney (1880) this population included two kinds of migrants: those for whom the illegality of entering the Hills was an added incentive and those who entered the Hills trying to pressure the government to make their entry legal by forcing the government to obtain the Hills by treaty or purchase (Newton and Jenney 1880:18). The 1880 Census of the United States listed the population of the Black Hills counties as 16,726, which excludes Indians. The 1890 Census reported 36,982 people in residence.

There were serious and predictable ramifications of defining the Black Hills as an open-access gold mine. There were no controls on who could come to the Hills or how they could use the land in the Black Hills. All activity centered on mining. Mining towns were boom towns with all activity oriented toward the discovery and extraction of gold. Word of a strike could cause one Black Hills town to become a ghost town and another to be born. The gold strike at Lead, S.D. led to settling the largest population center in the Hills, Lead/Deadwood (Fig.5a). Custer (see Fig.5b) was platted in 1875 before it was legal for whites to be in the area. Soon after the settlers were allowed back in, it was deserted by most of its population when a strike at Deadwood was reported. However, it did not become a ghost town because enough people remained to preserve its status as a viable county seat. Hill City was founded in the spring of 1876 when placer gold was found, but was deserted the same fall when gold was discovered in Deadwood (Wedge

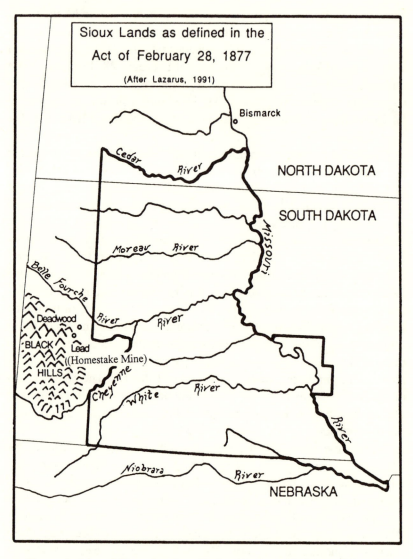

Figure 4. Map of Sioux Lands as Defined in Act of February 28, 1877

1979). It continued to follow a boom-and-bust pattern through this period, fueled by the Harney Peak Tin Mining, Milling and Manufacturing Company from 1883 to 1892, and hotel development by the Burlington Railroad beginning in 1892 (ibid.). In 1890 Hill City was booming with twenty-eight hundred men employed in and around the town (Wedge 1979:30).

All attention in the early boom towns focussed on the discovery of gold and no one paid attention to establishing permanent settlements. Houses were all made of wood and were not particularly carefully constructed, as evidenced by the fire that burned Deadwood in 1879 (Parker 1966).

Mining dominated the resource definition of timber, making it merely a subsidiary part of the definition of a mining field. Miners and other settlers cut trees for shelter, fuel, mine timbers, and sluices without regard for either the sustainability of the timber resource or the protective role a living forest plays against soil erosion, flood, and fire. Applying the same use pattern to timber as to gold, mining it as quickly and thoroughly as possible, denuded the Hills in the richest mining areas between Spearfish Creek and Elk Creek in the Northern Hills. The pattern of mining in this period was placer mining, a labor-and-water intensive method conducive to individual prospectors staking claims along streams. Consequently the trees along the streams were the first cut. Portable sawmills moved away from the streams as the tree line receded and demand remained steady. Damage was not reported at the time of the mining, but only after the Black Hills Forest Reserve was established and inspected. It is curious that stripping the trees from the

Figure 5a. Photo of Custer, S.D., 1904

Figure 5b. Photo of Lead, S. D. 1904

land was not mentioned in the contemporary descriptions of the mining boom. It was not until the *50th Anniversary History of the Black Hills National Forest* (1948) that there was a description of the degraded shape of the Forest at the time the Forest Reserve was established in 1898. Linde's (1984) description of the history of sawmills in the Black Hills also recounts that timber seemed so plentiful in the early days of settlement that conservation was never an issue. Sawmills existed to serve the needs of the miners. Since the Black Hills vegetation was new to Euro-Americans, no thought was given to the 40-year growing period of ponderosa pine.

The definition of "open access gold mine" included cattle as well as the precious metal because grass was considered gold above the ground. The same "boom or bust," "get rich quick" mentality that brought thousands of prospectors to the Hills attracted cattle barons, mostly from Texas, hoping to get rich running range cattle on grass they could obtain at little or no cost (Palais 1942:24). The first ranch was near the mining center of Deadwood in 1876, but after the area officially opened to white settlement and the Sioux were confined to reservations away from the Hills, more cattle ranchers brought large herds to capture both the mining business and the government business generated by furnishing rations to the Indians. In the early stages the cattle industry was the inverse of the mining industry; a few cattle ranchers dominated the industry with very large herds, while the mining industry started with many small-scale miners (Baldwin 1904:59). Outside capital funded the cattle industry and the object was to run as many cattle on the range as possible without regard for the condition of the range or protection the cattle might need in the winter. For ten years the cattle industry boomed; cattle cost $15 to $20 per head and could be sold for $100 to $125 in 1876. Investors expected a profit of 25–40 percent.

By 1883 there were five hundred thousand cattle in the Black Hills, and the range was severely overcrowded (Palais, 1942). The cattle barons made no effort to limit the stock on the range and continued to add cattle at every opportunity. They formed the Black Hills Livestock Association in 1880 to protect against thieves, fire, and wolves, and to conduct joint roundups in May with no mention of preserving or maintaining the range land.

The rigorous winter of 1886–87 was the undoing of the cattle industry. With a depleted range and too many cattle relying only on grass for food, winter conditions resulted in the loss of about 75 percent of the stock and was economically fatal to the speculatively financed corporations (Palais 1942:41). After that disaster the large herds disappeared and small-scale, mixed farming took over. Ironically, the number of cattle actually increased with small scale farmers, each with a hundred head or less, but they took a long-term interest in grazing land as a resource and the range conditions improved. They also learned that cattle could survive nicely on the Plains' grasses and summer pasture in the Black Hills, but stock owners found that it was not profitable to provide winter shelter. Consequently the trend in stock raising permanently changed to small herds rather than large herds (Baldwin 1904:61). Ironically, as the number of cattle grazers increased the number of miners decreased with the decline of placer mining.

The open-access period ended with a "tragedy of the commons" in the Hardin sense. Depletion of timber and resulting damage to the watershed resource occurred in the process of exploiting the gold resource, but were not considered problems because there was never a time when the Black Hills was in danger of losing all of its forests. When one area around a mine was depleted, the miners could move the sawmills or start a new mine. Gold, timber, and grazing land were open-access resources, used by all who wanted them without regard to their continued viability. The fact that gold was the resource the prospectors were after does not diminish the impact of the damage to the forest or the range. These tragedies of the commons had all occurred on publicly held land.

The open-access gold mine period was distinctly different from a common property resource (CPR) management scheme. There were no qualifications for membership in the group eligible to use the resource; it was open to all. There was also no management plan aimed at the perpetuation of any of the resources involved in the gold mining. Anyone could use the resources in any way they wanted to use them and the result was nonsustainable resource use.

Defining a Goverment-Owned Forest 1897 to 1905: Creating the Forest Reserve

The creation of the forest reserve was an intentional resource redefinition. The Black Hills Forest Reserve was located in a place where people had already settled and assigned a resource definition incompatible with the government goal of preserving the nation's forest resources. There had to be both a redefinition of the resource and a recharacterization of the nature of public ownership. The process of establishing government control involved demonstrating the government's authority to the existing population. This period lasted from the creation of the reserve in 1897 until approximately 1905 when the control of the Reserve was transferred from the Department of the Interior to the Department of Agriculture.

President Cleveland's eleventh-hour proclamation on February 22, 1897, creating the Black Hills Forest Reserve along with several other western reserves, was not a popular event in the Black Hills. People living there were invested in maintaining the resource definition that was in effect prior to creation of the Reserve. Most of them benefited from that definition and had probably been drawn to the area because of the open-access gold mine definition.

The settlers of the Black Hills vigorously protested the establishment of the Black Hills Forest Reserve when they learned of it from Eastern newspapers. The proclamation issued on February 22, 1897 reached the Hills by telegram and within four days, the protest had been set in motion. The *Rapid City Journal* reported "telegrams and letters of remonstrance being sent in by the hundreds and public meetings being held" (RCJ 26 February 1897, p.1). There was a widespread belief that since all of the Western congressmen opposed the reserves, they would be "nullified" (RCJ 27 February 1897, p. 1).

Some cooler heads were skeptical that the forest reserves would actually cause the demise of the West even if they were established. The *Rapid City Journal* ran a front-page story on March 2, 1897 saying that the forest reserve would not have adverse consequences since it did not alter rights of location and entry on mineral land guaranteed by the Mining Law of 1872 and the Forest Reserve Act of 1891. Such rationality quickly gave way to public opinion and support for the Senate's prompt (March 3, 1897) action to stay Cleveland's proclamation until further study could be made under President McKinley. This change in reporting from a rational, factual presentation of the terms of the forest reserve proclamation and its consequences for people living in the Black Hills, to editorials condemning the action and supporting the protest, suggests that the editorial policy of the *Rapid City Journal* reflected the interests of the business community, even when the business community did not stick with the facts. None of the newspaper accounts even hinted at a possible reason for establishing Forest Reserves. The arguments against the Forest Reserves were that they would arrest development of the area by keeping homesteaders out and preventing mining.

A weekly feature entitled "A Few Facts and Figures" appeared in the *Rapid City Journal* throughout the mid- and late 1890s. While this article was a puff piece somewhere between a straight promotional article for prospective settlers and an educational article on the natural history and current economy of the Black Hills, it does give some insight into the way the forest was viewed locally. Timber resources were described only in terms of production. The article boasts of "large mills producing the best of native lumber being produced at about one-half the price the same lumber is to be had in Omaha and other eastern markets" (RCJ 27 January 1897, p. 1). From this article one would expect that even after twenty years of settlement virgin forests still abounded. The same article reports that in the twenty years gold had been mined, $110 million worth had been produced in the Black Hills. An abundance of other minerals was also reported, so the mining aspect of the definition of the Hills was expanding. The Black Hills were clearly valued for their economic production. Later (post-1905) accounts of the establishment of the Black Hills Forest Reserve provide the only clues about the condition of the forest.

Who comprised the public so outraged at the creation of the Forest Reserve? The censuses for the region provide a glimpse of both the population distribution and natural resource use during this period. The 1905 South Dakota census provides the best information on the region. Wyoming did not do a state census, so the 1890 federal census information is used for Crook and Weston Counties. Using 1905 census data has a few drawbacks, but it was the best source available on length of time people had lived in South Dakota, their distribution within the Black Hills study area, and the predominant occupations. These figures coincide with the historical descriptions of the populations and economic activities reported in Black Hills town histories. The pre-Reserve settlement patterns really dictated the boundaries of the National Forest and the resource definition that could be applied to it. The southern counties were much more agriculturally oriented than the northern counties that were dominated by mining companies. In Custer County, which was almost completely contained within the Forest Reserve boundaries, the majority of the people lived in unclassified townships. This residential pattern would be consistent with homesteading. In Fall River almost half lived in Hot Springs and most lived in organized towns. By 1905 Hot Springs was a thriving health resort capitalizing on the warm mineral springs as a healing mecca. Fall River County is the southern most county and the forest itself did not extend into much of it. In Lawrence County, the towns of Lead, Deadwood, and Spearfish accounted for most of the population with only about 12 percent living in unnamed or unclassified townships. This pattern would be consistent with mining. Deadwood was the leading town in the Hills and the center of much of the gambling, drinking, and gunfighting that the Old West was famous for. In Meade County, which contained both plains and forest, most of the people lived in unnamed or unclassified townships. Rapid City dominated Pennington County. It was called the "Gateway City" because it occupied the midpoint of the north-south axis of the Black Hills, but it did not have the population of Deadwood and Lead.

This distribution within counties combined with the occupation information reflects the different resource definition in the various counties. In Custer, Fall River and Meade Counties the top three occupations for men were farmers, ranchers, laborers and agricultural laborers. Custer had only 78 miners, Fall River 3 and Meade 9. In Lawrence County the greatest occupation was mining, with twenty-seven hundred miners and farming was the next closest category with 545. Only thirty-five men called themselves ranchers in Lawrence County. In Pennington County farmers were the largest occupation group (444), laborers (314), railroad workers (274), and miners (216). The overwhelming occupation reported for women in all counties was housewife. One drawback of the single occupation reporting system was that it did not capture true situation that most people engaged in aspects of several occupations.

The relative stability of the population within the Black Hills is reflected by the 1905 census figures on the length of time people had lived in South Dakota. Length of time in the county of residence is not available, so length of time in South Dakota is used as the best available information. By 1905 over half of the population of Custer, Fall River, Meade, and Pennington Counties had lived in South Dakota more than ten years, while in Lawrence County 61 percent had lived in South Dakota less than ten years. If the children under the age of ten are excluded from the comparison, Lawrence still has 50 percent of the population living in South Dakota less than ten years. This may reflect a fairly stable population in the southern Hills, but a less stable population in the northern Hills by 1905, which would be consistent with the mining in the north and farming/homesteading in the south.

Gaining Public Support for the National Forest

The government's first task after declaration of the Forest Reserve was to gain the support of the Black Hills public by educating them about the definition and purpose of a forest reserve. The Department of the Interior did not want to eliminate the mining resource definition, only to broaden it to include timber and the watershed. They went to great lengths to affirm the primary importance of the mining industry and to educate the public and the mining industry that a well-maintained forest reserve would greatly benefit the mining industry. Probably for political reasons, the Department of the Interior did not harp on the poor condition of the Black Hills forests, but instead emphasized how beneficial a forest reserve would be, announcing, "The object of this timber reservation is to preserve the timber for the benefit of the mining industry conceded to be the leading industry of the Hills . . ." (RCJ 10 September 1898, p.1). Indeed the Act of June 4, 1897 (30 Statutes, 36) that created forest reserves specifically reserved the right of any person to enter upon a forest reservation "for all proper and lawful purposes, including that of prospecting, locating and developing the mineral resources thereon." Additionally, the mineral resources had been the reason for taking the land from the Sioux, so the government was certainly not going to ban mining after it had gained control.

Asserting Control through Challenges to Private Ownership

The creation of the reserve froze property rights as of September 18, 1898, meaning that homesteads established and towns organized by that date remained private property. The northern Hills were predominantly populated by miners who lived in organized towns, while the southern Hills were predominantly populated by farmers who lived on homesteads dispersed throughout the Forest. The Department of the Interior was in the position of a buyer of an estate with many tenants. The first thing the buyer had to do was survey the estate and make sure all the tenants were in line. In this case, because of the characteristics of the Black Hills population and the statutory parameters of the forest reserves, the government concentrated its efforts to establish ownership by examining mining and homestead claims and regulating timber and grazing. In this examination the government was guided by complementary missions: 1) to support the mining industry and 2) to use the Black Hills Forest Reserve as a model working forest in which timber, mining, and grazing all complemented each other. The government began its assertion of control by examining mining claims and homesteads for their legitimacy. Next, they asserted regulatory control over timber cutting and grazing rights.

Examination of mining claims was important because there was a perception that many mining claims were filed fraudulently. While the government could not, and did not want to prevent legitimate mining within national forest reserves, they did have the power to challenge individual claims. The mining industry had no complaint about this as long as the government went after individuals' claims filed without the requisite discovery for speculation purposes, avoiding the freeze on homesteading within the forest boundaries or merely to cut good timber. By this time mining companies had supplanted placer mining and mining companies had no objection to individual prospectors being bothered by the government. In 1904 the Black Hills Mining Association published what was essentially a prospectus on the mining industry in the Black Hills (Baldwin 1904). The book's subtitle was "A Terse Description of Conditions Past and Present of AMERICA'S GREATEST MINERAL BELT, Its Agricultural and Cattle Resources, Principal Cities, Financial, Commercial, Educational and Religious Institutions, Railways, Scenery and Health and Pleasure Resorts". This book not only catalogues a large number of mines in 1904, but was prepared for the express purpose of getting investors to put capital in Black Hills enterprises. The Black Hills Mining Men's Association did not consider the inspection of mines a threat, because all mines that produced some sort of mineral were protected by the Mining Act of 1872 and reaffirmed in the Organic Act of 1897 which launched the national forest reserves.

Examination and regulation of homesteads was another way in which the government exerted its ownership. However, there was not as much public support for examination of homesteads and the process did not go as smoothly as examining mining claims had gone. Homesteaders within the reserve at the time it was created were allowed to remain, but after the creation date no new homesteads were allowed.

Homesteads were explicitly confined to agricultural land and the conflicts centered on whether the land claimed was more suitable for mining or timber than for agriculture. Homesteads allowed for more land to be claimed than did mining claims. The temptation was to claim 160 acres as a homestead, hoping that there would be mining strikes under it. Mining claims were restricted to areas where minerals actually existed. Other miners could stake claims in the vicinity of a successful strike, but if a homestead was patented, the land could not be mined by anyone other than the homesteader. The Department of Interior investigated the homesteads existing at the time of the establishment of the Reserve to see whether they were bona fide homesteads or filed for speculative or fraudulent purposes (RCJ 15 November 1903, p.1). Homesteads established between the 1897 initial announcement of the creation of the forest reserve and the actual implementation of the reserve in 1898 were examined particularly closely.

At the beginning of this period, the government exerted its ownership by challenging homesteads not filed properly. There was a ninety day period in which homesteaders were required to file their claims after a township was platted. However, platting of the township was not always well publicized and some homesteaders did not understand the requirement. Homesteaders who failed to meet that deadline had their claims disqualified by the General Land Office of the Department of Interior. The government's use of this legal technicality caused a great furor in the Hills because some of the homesteaders had been on "their" land for fifteen to twenty years or they were second-generation homesteaders who had purchased their land from the original homesteaders who had not perfected their title. The solution was to approach Congress for a legislative remedy. Congress was very willing to assist by waiving the ninety-day filing requirement for people who settled the land in good faith and through some type of excusable neglect had failed to perfect their title. In the process of the congressional action, there was much public discussion of what upstanding citizens had settled the Black Hills and how it would be inequitable to oust them from the land. They were the type of people the government should support. (See for example, RCJ 3 October 1901, p.1, 4 October 1901, p.1, 12 April 1902, p.1, 1 June 1902, p.1, 30 December 1903, p.1.) Objections to the homestead relief measures were mostly made by holders of large tracts of fine timber held under mineral leases. Miners and bona fide settlers had no conflict with the Department of the Interior on this issue because of the supportive role farming played with regard to mining (RCJ

22 December 1903, p.1). They did not want the Homestead Act used to establish either timber or mining empires.

Asserting Control through Regulation of Activity

Timber Regulation

Regulation of timber cutting was the most effective means of asserting government control over the forest reserve. Timber was the reason for establishing the reserve and was the resource element that most needed protection. Regulation of timber cutting was an "ownership-defining" event because it could no longer be an open-access resource. All cutting needed to be scrutinized.

The primary regulating device was the application procedure. "Case Number 1" set the tone for the relationship between the government and the mining industry in the Black Hills and established the timber sale procedure nationwide. This 1898 sale of timber to Homestake Mining Company in the northern Hills was the first sale of timber to the private sector from a forest reserve. Before the creation of the reserve Homestake had been cutting timber and needed to continue to use timber to support its mining operations. Homestake's early timber-cutting habits were in fact responsible for much of the deforestation around Lead, Deadwood, and Spearfish. Homestake owned much of the land in the northern Hills that was not in the forest reserve because it no longer had trees on it. Homestake was the major employer in the region as well as the major source of economic well-being for the region.

Figures 6a through 6d capture some of the flavor of the early mining practices. Fig.6a shows a flume built to carry timber to the mines; Fig. 6b shows the Columbia mine in the early 1900s, a especially shows the deforestation of the area; Figure 6c shows a small boy at the entrance of a mine. When these figures are compared with Fig.6d, The Homestake Mine, it is clear that Homestake was much larger than the other mining operations.

The first question after creation of the reserve was whether Homestake Mine would use its substantial financial and political resources to challenge the reserve or accept the government's authority to establish it. Homestake's willingness to work with the Department of the Interior set a tone for mutual respect between the mining industry and the new owners of the timber, the government. Initially there was no procedure for selling timber and yet it was clear that if the government did not start to sell timber, the mining industry would suffer and probably force a confrontation over the existence of forest reserves. The government and

Figure 6a. Flume for mine timbers

Homestake were able to negotiate a procedure for selling timber to private industries that became the standard for all forest reserves.

Creation of the application procedure was partly a cure for the problem of furnishing timber to the mining industry and partly a problem in itself. There had been no inventory of timber at the time of the creation of the Forest Reserve; there was barely a boundary survey in 1897. The Department of the Interior did not have enough staff to effectively manage the reserve and this caused problems with the application procedure. Permits were rather freely granted in the first years, but permittees took advantage of the situation and behaved as if timber was still an open access resource. In 1900 the Supervisor of the Forest Reserve said that it was not going to be as easy as it used to be to get a permit

Figure 6b. Columbia Mine early 1900s

because it was suspected that there had been a lot of speculation in past timber sales caused at least in part by the lack of an inventory and understaffing of the Forest Reserve. In 1900 there were only eight forest rangers for the whole forest. In March 1900 an official was sent from the Forestry Division of the Department of Agriculture to determine the merchantable timber in the Black Hills in order to speed up the timber sale process. The application procedure had been taking ninety days, a period that was considered too long (RCJ 31 March 1900, p.1). Several sawmills went out of business waiting for timber permits. Through the inventory and tighter application procedure the government established a very visible ownership presence.

Grazing Regulation

Regulation of grazing rights was another way in which the government took control. Leasing of grazing land was a major concern throughout the western states, including the Black Hills region. Forest reserve grazing was very important for cattle and horses in the Black Hills region because of the protection from heat, access to water (even in the summer) and good pasture found in the Forest. Two aspects of the government's regulation are particularly important: 1) the decision to favor small grazing leases, and 2) the decision to ban sheep from the Reserve.

The quality of grazing land was a problem that carried over from the

Figure 6c. Mine with Boy

Figure 6d. Homestake Mine, Lead, S.D.

earlier open-access grazing period. Between 1885 and 1901, the cattle range in the Black Hills area had diminished 81 percent and many people were calling for a recuperative period. (RCJ 9 January 1903, p.1). In 1900 the debate was over whether Congress should allow leases by large companies as well as by individuals. Sentiment in the Black Hills strongly favored small leases. Several articles in February 1900 (RCJ 17 February 1900, p.1 and 27 February 1900, p.1) called on small stockmen to oppose the granting of leases in the thousands of acres because large companies would get the best land and ruin it by overstocking. People needed only to look back at the cattle industry before the winter of 1886 to 1887 to realize that such a situation had already existed in the Black Hills. This concern was addressed by implementing grazing regulations in the national forest that gave preference to residents within the reserve who owned fewer than one hundred head of horses or cattle.

Regulations were issued in 1902 governing the permit procedure. The order of grazing permit preference was: 1) residents of the reserve; 2) stock of persons owning ranches within the reserve, but residing outside the reserve; 3) stock of persons living in the immediate vicinity of the reserve (called "neighboring stock") and 4) stock of "outsiders who have some equitable claim" (RCJ 26 February 1902, p.1). These preferences were designed to favor small stock holders and keep the large companies out of the reserves.

The Black Hills area was no different than the rest of the West when it came to cattle and sheep conflicts. Reports of conflict between the two interests were commonplace in the *Rapid City Journal* as illustrated by this September 21, 1898 story.

> A company of cattlemen visited Mr. Fuhrman near French Creek last week and requested him to move his sheep back to his own range, but he refused to do so, whereupon they hitched their saddle ropes to the wagon and moved it and the sheep through Fairburn to his own place. We understand he went to Custer the next day to see if he couldn't have the cattlemen arrested.

No later arrest was reported.

Irrespective of that prejudice, sheep were an important part of the local economy. It was estimated in 1903 that there were 300,000 head of cattle, 100,000 head of sheep and 7,000 head of horses grazing in the Black Hills vicinity, though not all in the Forest Reserve (Baldwin 1904:63). Sheep growers cooperated with each other. They built warehouses to store wool, allowing them to send the wool to market when the price was best. Although much of the sheep industry was centered on Belle Fourche, north of the Forest Reserve, all of the Black Hills counties reported substantial sheep populations in the 1905 state census. The wool warehouse in Rapid City, servicing area counties, even shipped more wool than the Belle Fourche warehouse in 1900.

Given its substantial economic presence in the Black Hills, the decision to prohibit sheep from the forest reserve came under some criticism. It was suggested by one member of the Cleveland administration in 1902 that forest reserves should either be cut down or the rules changed to allow sheep to avoid annihilating the entire wool-growing industry (RCJ 30 December 1902, p.1). The decision to ban sheep continued throughout this period. It was essentially a political decision and one the government could enforce because it owned the reserve. The Department of the Interior did not change the ban on sheep in the reserves.

Protecting Land by Fencing

Another problem during the early days of the forest reserve was private appropriation of public lands. The issue surfaced through challenges to fencing land. The Department of the Interior in 1902 began a "get tough" policy about fences on the public domain. Until then the government had winked at fences, but beginning July 1, 1902, extra enforcement agents were deployed to take down fences. In the Black Hills the fences were more for protecting garden crops than for corralling cattle or claiming exclusive rights to grazing land. Since cattle grazed unfenced in the forest reserve, fencing the crops was the only protection. By getting tough on the fencing issue, the government was again asserting its ownership.

Mining Reigns Supreme

The Black Hills remained a mining resource even after the forest reserve had been established. The overall definition of the forest as an open-access mining resource did not change substantially in this period. Congress was actively encouraging mining research (RCJ, 10 March 1900, p.1). South Dakota adopted liberal mining laws making it a friendly place for mining companies to incorporate. Mine owners in the Black Hills formed the Black Hills Mining Men's Association in 1901 primarily for the purpose of getting outside capital to finance mining ventures in the Hills (McFarland 1904). Among the association's early accomplishments was securing the American Mining Congress meeting for Deadwood and Lead in 1902. The exposure from this congress helped raise venture capital for the area. The association acted as a clearinghouse for information on the Black Hills, responding to inquiries about mining opportunities. The 1904 *Black Hills Illustrated* described 147 mining companies in Lawrence, Pennington, and Custer Counties, listing the extent of their claim and how one could invest in them (Baldwin 1904). Mining was a pervasive activity throughout the Hills.

Gold still reigned supreme as the object of mining activity, but other minerals gained in importance. A November 14, 1900 article in the *Rapid City Journal* discussed the state of mining in the Black Hills. It reported the following mining products: mica, marble, kaolin clay, onyx stone, lithograph stone, paint pigment, iron and gold ore, and tin from Custer County; tin, gold, silver, iron, spodumene, and copper from Pennington County; and gold, silver, lead wolframite, tin, copper, and iron from Lawrence County. Investments to support the mining industry came mostly from outside capital in the East, Colorado, and California. One of the necessities of mining was to have a market. In this period the trend seemed to be that minerals would be identified and then uses for them sought. For example, in the January 16, 1900 *Rapid City Journal* attempts to develop the mineral spodumene found in Pennington County as a stomach treatment were reported. No market or great spodumene industry was reported.

The primacy of mining was obvious in several other ways. In 1902, Seth Bullock, Supervisor of the Black Hills Forest Reserve, tried to get a school of forestry established at the South Dakota School of Mines located in Rapid City, but because of the dominance of the mining interest, the idea died in its infancy (RCJ 17 May 1910, p.1). Forest reserve timber could only be sold within the state where the reserve was located. In the case of the Black Hills Forest Reserve, this ensured that the timber would be used to support the mining industry. Forest roads, constructed to serve as the infrastructure for maintaining the forest, were appropriated by the mining interests to be part of their infrastructure. In 1904 a forest ranger decided to repair a forest road from Placereville to Canyon City, but not from Mystic to Silver City because the latter route was not important for forest purposes. An editorial in the *Rapid City Journal* branded the decision ridiculous because mining machinery would have to be unloaded at Hill City and carried to the northern Hills, causing delays for the mining companies. The editor accused the forest ranger of using his office to the point of petty tyranny (RCJ 27 March

1904, p.1), but perhaps his worst crime was failing to understand the supremacy of mining.

That the Hills were a mining resource is also evident from the way in which the preservation of other natural resources was subordinated to mining. As the most accessible types of gold were mined, chemical processes were needed to extract gold from ore. The deep refractory ore was very difficult to extract; the most effective process developed was the cyanide process introduced in the 1890s (Parker 1966:193). This process "dissolved the gold from the ore with either potassium or sodium cyanide, and made possible utilization of many gold deposits previously considered totally unprofitable" (ibid.). In September and October 1901 the first cyanide plants were established in the Black Hills, first at the Homestake Mine and then in Rapid City. Cyanide was an efficient way to extract gold from ore, but the waste was toxic. The cyanide plants discharged their waste into streams from the beginning, as was the custom with waste disposal at the time. Because the cyanide was so toxic to the aquatic environment and poisoned the water supply for all downstream, there were complaints about pollution from the first use of cyanide. The complaints included the poisoning of livestock as well as fish. Even farmers who found their fields turned to cement after a flood found no relief, even through the courts. It was profitable enough to the mining industries to outweigh the criticism.

Development of the Black Hills benefited greatly from the mining emphasis. Intra-Black Hills railroads were in place long before outside lines because of the necessity for good transportation within the Hills to support the mining industry. (See Figure 7.) By 1901 Burlington Railroad had a standard gauge line into Lead (RCJ 18 October 1901, p.1). Rapid City lobbied heavily to be the terminus for various railroad building ventures as gateway to the Hills, and it was centrally located to service both the northern and southern reaches of the Hills. The Burlington Railroad was a full partner in development of the region, willing to build railroads wherever business led it since it entered the Hills in 1892 (RCJ 10 May 1900, p.1).

Results of the Definition Change

By 1904 the Black Hills Forest Reserve was no longer an open-access timber or grazing resource. The government had regulations in place to control access and to monitor use of those resource elements. There were still instances of illegal cutting, but a rudimentary process was in

Figure 7. Missouri and Pacific Railroad Servicing Mines, early 1900s

place to prosecute offenders. Using the government power to prosecute people who cut timber illegally was not popular when it was used against mining companies. Public sentiment ran heavily against the government in suits against mining companies for overcutting. The government was also seen as overbearing when it was prosecuting mining companies (RCJ 22 January 1898, p.1). There was a moratorium on homesteading within the forest boundaries so the land rush had stopped. In these ways the government had established its ownership presence.

Government ownership was emphasized so much that a kind of land-lord/tenant relationship was established between the Department of the Interior and the forest users. As in most such relationships the tenant expected the landlord to perform the maintenance duties. Holders of grazing leases or timber permits acted in their own immediate self interest because it was the government's property they were trying to make a profit from. The Department of Interior could not staff the Forest adequately to mark cuts, police activity, or even deal with the scourges of all forests, fires and insects. The staffing levels were woefully inadequate for even one of those tasks. Although the level of forest degradation had slowed from prior to establishment of the forest reserve, the Department of the Interior was not able to do more than barely slow the process. All of the rules and regulations came from the top down, with no input from forest users.

Merely establishing government ownership over the forest reserve was insufficient to change its definition from a mining resource, or to build a community that felt responsible for taking care of the forest. However, there was still a strong desire among conservationists, led by Gifford Pinchot, the Forester for the Department of Agriculture, to establish a multiple-use working forest in the European tradition of local management and control. The Department of the Interior was unable to accomplish this task. Transfer of responsibility for the forest reserves to the Department of Agriculture under Gifford Pinchot began the new stage of resource redefinition.

As shown in Figure 8, the BHNF sign signifies the change from the Department of the Interior to the Department of Agriculture.

Figure 8. Black Hills National Forest near Rapid City

Chapter 3

The Simple Common Property Resource Period, 1905 to 1919

By the end of the first years of the Black Hills National Forest under the Department of Interior, it was evident that the forest could not be managed solely by government employees isolated from the local populace. The forest was too vast to be policed effectively by the small number of officials the government could afford. Also, the local populace already had established use patterns in the forest that had proven detrimental. In 1905 authority for the National Forests was transferred from the Department of the Interior to the Department of Agriculture by Congress, and both definitional and managerial changes commenced. The Department of Agriculture did not explicitly say "the Black Hills National Forest will henceforth be a common property resource." Rather, the Department of Agriculture began to redefine the forest as a multiple-use resource and to intentionally involve local people in its management. The change was in line with President Theodore Roosevelt's conservationist position and represented an opportunity for Pinchot and Roosevelt to team up to implement a conservation policy in the western United States. President Roosevelt owned a ranch in North Dakota and was very interested in having the West developed within the conservation model.

This first common property resource period could be called "the simple common property period" because of its relatively uncomplicated structure compared to the later common property period in the 1970s and 1980s. In this first period, the uses were clearly defined as watershed protection, timber, mining, and recreation. The population was small enough and the forest was big enough to allow uses to coexist without directly conflicting with each other. Some accommodation among users and uses was necessary, but there was no sense that resources were scarce. Users generally took advantage of more than one aspect of the multiple-use definition.

This chapter describes the simple common property period in terms of the three elements of a common property resource scheme: a clearly defined resource, an identified group of people with the right to use the resource, and an accepted management plan to assure the continued existence of the resource.

Redefining the Black Hills National Forest as a Resource

The national debate in the early 1900s over the meaning of natural resource conservation had a great deal of influence on the redefinition of the Black Hills National Forest as a resource. Within the federal government, there were two levels of debate about the forest reserves: a continuous debate involving the western states about state versus federal control of resources, and a debate over whether the forest should be developed or preserved. During this period, state's rights and differences in natural resource philosophy were intertwined. The debate over state versus federal control has never really been resolved, although South Dakota and Wyoming acquiesced in the existence of the Black Hills National Forest. The conservation policy embodied in the multiple-use concept was not a popular one in the western states, and an adversarial relationship between the federal government and the population living in the forest had developed. Westerners did not come out against conservation per se, but they said they wanted sane conservation (use of resources) and Pinchot's version was not sane (RCJ 14 September 1910, p.1; 12 April 1914, p.1; 22 September 1915 p.1). On more than one occasion Gifford Pinchot was described as the worst calamity that ever struck the western states (RCJ 19 February 1914, p.1).

Part of the debate over the meaning of conservation focused on whether the Department of the Interior or the Department of Agriculture should be in control of the forest reserves. Gifford Pinchot was a major figure in this debate. He literally was the forestry department of the Department of Agriculture and lobbied hard for President Theodore Roosevelt to transfer control of the forests to the Department of Agriculture. The Department of the Interior had taken a preservationist view toward the forest reserves. Interior had defined its mission as assessing and repairing the damage done to the forest in the first 20 years of United States occupation and establishing government control over its use. By the end of the period, the government had cracked down on wholesale cutting of trees, replanted much of the deforested area, done a cursory survey of the area, and established rules and regulations about forest use. Pinchot wanted a multiple-use forest, in the European sense, and consequently, when the forest reserves came under the jurisdiction of the Department of Agriculture in early 1905, that department took a more expansive view of the forest as a resource than the Department of Interior had taken.

Gifford Pinchot was particularly interested in the Black Hills National Forest because of his visits to the area and because of President Roosevelt's connections with the Black Hills. When the national forests came under his jurisdiction he chose the Black Hills National Forest to be a model multiple-use forest and a place of experimentation (Pinchot 1947). Despite its development as a mining area, the Black Hills forest lends itself well to multiple use. It not only has rich mining resources and timber but also has agricultural land interspersing the timber areas in natural parks. The Black Hills National Forest could easily accommodate all of Pinchot's desired multiple uses (which were also written into the statutes): timber harvest, mining, grazing and recreation. The uses were further defined by the local context: timber harvest was aimed at servicing the needs of the mining industry; mining included extracting known deposits of minerals and looking for any potentially useful mineral; grazing referred only to cattle and horses; and, recreation consisted mostly of enjoying the tranquility of the forest and trout fishing. It was during this period that yellow ponderosa pine was chosen as the species of choice for the Reserve. Experts from Yale University who came to inspect new seeding methods suggested that all future reseeding efforts be confined to yellow pine because it flourished so well (RCJ 7 November 1907, p.1). Tensions among these uses are discussed later in the user and management section.

Creating the Forest Community

The government did not have enough funds to take care of the forest without the cooperation and investment of the local population. Fostering a forest community was essential to both changing the resource definition of the forest and maintaining the forest. The people already living on the forest would have been the logical core of any forest community, but at the beginning of this period they were in an adversarial relationship with the government. Seth Bullock was of major assistance in establishing the Black Hills National Forest. Bullock was part of the first provisional government in the Northern Black Hills to protect mining interests (Parker 94), was a no-nonsense sheriff (ibid. 174), and was also related by marriage to the owner of Homestake Mines. Pinchot appointed him the first supervisor of the Black Hills National Forest, setting the pattern for insisting on local control of the forest through the hiring of only local men as forest rangers (Pinchot 1947). It was Bullock's position that the local community should be responsible for and benefit from the national forest. Through local control, some of the hostility toward existence of the national forest was dissipated. In addition to hiring local men as rangers, the local community was consulted about management policy.

However, local control was not the entire answer because the population of the BHNF was understandably dominated by people invested in the old definition of the Forest as a mine. In order to begin to change the resource definition of the reserve from a mining area to a multiple-use forest, the population of the forest had to change. The process of changing the forest population began by determining whether the existing residents could stay or would have to leave and allow recruiting migrants to implement the new resource definition. Another part of the process was clearly defining the boundaries of the forest community on the basis of use in addition to residence. Building a forest community was a multi-phased, intentional process.

Sorting Out Illegal Forest Homesteaders

At the beginning of this first common property period the forest community consisted of miners, lumbermen, legal homesteaders who arrived before 1898, and illegal homesteaders who arrived after 1898. One of the early tasks was to cull the ranks of the forest residents, legitimize those who fit in with the redefinition plan, and eliminate those whose presence compromised the plan.

People who had homesteaded on what became the Black Hills Forest Reserve before the creation of the reserve in 1898 were legal residents of the Forest Reserve. Even though the Reserve land was closed to homesteading after 1898, people continued to settle on the land. By the beginning of this period there were a considerable number of illegal homesteaders on the forest. Their presence was known to the government, but no definitive action had been taken to evict or to legitimize them. One Department of the Interior policy had been aimed at making their life difficult. Fences were permitted on private land within the Reserve, but not on public land. Since the illegal homesteaders did not have title to their land, they were occupying public land. One of the last acts of the Department of the Interior was to enforce the government ban on fencing on public land which was tantamount to eviction because the homesteaders could not protect their crops. In July 1905, a hundred men who were living on the forest, but did not have title to the land they were occupying, met to form the Black Hills Forest Reserve Homebuilders Association for the purpose of asking Congress to help them get title to their land. They asked Congress to be allowed to "prove up" (pay money showing their intention to stay on the land) at $2.50 per acre. Seth Bullock, Supervisor of the BHNF, attended the meeting and supported their request (RCJ 6 July 1905, p.1). These homesteaders, even though they were illegal, fit into the plan for encouraging settlement within the Reserve and were legitimized as part of the forest community.

Another type of illegal homesteaders, miners making spurious claims, was not welcomed into the forest community. A considerable number of mining claims were turned into settlement opportunities and the Forest Service made it a priority to inspect mining claims and determine which were legitimate and which were really claims for settlement purposes (RCJ 12 December 1906, p.1; 22 January 1907, p.1; 3 March 1907, p.1). Whether people were evicted from their claims or not depended to some degree on how valuable their illegitimate use of the claim site was to the community. For example, running a hunting and fishing lodge from a mining site was allowed by a court, but using a mining claim as a recreational cabin site was not allowed (RCJ 21 December 1906, p.1).

Adding Agriculturalists

Another example of intentional community building was fostering migration of agricultural migrants to the forest. The original statute allowing the creation of the Black Hills Forest Reserve stated reserves could not contain land that was more useful for agriculture than for timber (Act of June 4, 1897, 30 Statutory Law 11, 34). However, all agricultural land in the Black Hills had not been claimed by the time the Reserve was set aside and legal settlement was suspended. Establishing a community committed to multiple use of the forest was made much easier by passage of the Forest Homestead Act of 1906 (Act of June 11, 1906) which reopened agricultural lands within the Forest Reserves to homesteaders. The Forest Homestead Act satisfied two groups: the people who wanted as little land as possible in federal hands and the forest service that desperately needed help managing the reserve. Having more homesteaders in the forest also increased its multiple use by adding grazers and timber users, and it added manpower to help protect against fires, help fight fires, police illegal cutting, and generally act like guardians of the forest.

The problem was that while the land opened to homesteading was technically agricultural, the climate was inhospitable and it was very difficult to keep homesteaders on the land. However, it was important enough to have agriculturalists on the land that the government made many amendments to the homesteading rules to prevent disqualifications. For instance, fourteen months of continuous residence was required, but when the severe Black Hills winters forced many homesteaders to abandon their claims, Congress amended the requirements to allow for a leave of absence of three months during the winter. The idea was to promote agricultural use as a goal of its own, not just as a supplement to mining and the only way to do that was to encourage migration.

Also it was recognized that an agricultural population would be more stable than a mining population that responded to boom-and-bust mining cycles very quickly, leaving numerous ghost towns in their wake. While this sponsored migration did result in a substantial increase in the population of the Hills region and greater use of the Black Hills National Forest for agriculture, not all agricultural land was taken. One of the advantages of government sponsorship was that the Forest Service treated these homesteaders as the core of the forest community. Many homesteaders were from east of the Mississippi, and they were welcomed with open arms and with great expectations that they were prosperous farmers coming to turn the area into an agricultural region (RCJ 4 September 1906, p.1). The Forest Service's commitment to homesteaders was evident in this statement reported in the *Rapid City Journal* on October 1, 1913:

> It is the aim of local forest officers to render all possible assistance to prospective settlers, in that their presence is of considerable value in not only assisting in the prevention and fighting of forest fires but also in bringing about a more complete utilization of the natural resources within the national forests. (p.1)

Adding Recreationists

Another intentional change fostered by the Department of Agriculture was to add a stable recreation group to the forest community. People living in the Black Hills towns had been using the Hills for recreation long before this period started. Many had built recreational cabins in secluded spots, or in good hunting or fishing areas. When the Department of Agriculture took over, they really had a choice of whether they would try to evict the summer residents of the forest or legitimize them. They increased the multiple use and helped conserve forest resources by encouraging summer residents. Summer recreationists helped the Forest Service by providing additional fire protection and by being watchful of other uses of the forest, especially illegal cutting. Their presence was legitimized with a forest leasing law in 1915 (part of the 1916 Department of Agriculture appropriation). The forest leasing law allowed for thirty-year leases on five-acre lots for summer homes, hotels, stores and public conveniences. No patents were issued and the lots were not to be used for homesteads. One interesting part of the law was that "responsible people and organizations" were eligible for the permits. Nowhere in the regulations or Forest Service rules was there a description of what was a responsible person or organization. Most of the rules had to do with the kind of building that could be erected and fire control. The intent of the law was to enlarge the usefulness of the forest for recreational purposes (RCJ 19 March 1915, p.1).

Hunting and trout fishing were the main outdoor recreational activities. Both the year-round population and the summer recreationists supported those activities as legitimate recreation and legitimate use of the forest (RCJ 10 September 1910, p.1; 8 October 1913, p.1). Recreationists welcomed into the forest community included local residents of the forest and area communities and tourism promoters, especially railroads.

The railroads were a particularly big factor in promoting both migration and tourism (Chicago and NorthWestern Railway 1916). In the first ten years of mining in the Black Hills, heavy mining equipment was hauled to the Hills by ox teams or bull teams from the last stop on the railroad somewhere east of the Missouri River (Fielder 1964:8). The ox teams left their mark on the landscape because they required wide main streets to make their turnaround at the end of trek in Custer or Rapid City. They were also slow, but they were the only way to get the materials to set up an intra-Hills narrow gauge mining railroad system. Once the standard guage railroads started to service the Hills from Chicago or St. Louis, they needed to do more than carry mining machinery one way and ore the other. Tourism and migration were publicity priorities for the railroads. They offered special packages to all of the scenic spots in the Hills, not just the National Forest. Hot Springs was promoted as a health resort (NorthWestern Line 1910), the Wild West atmosphere of Deadwood was promoted as something to see. The railroads advertised the existence of homesteads and offered good rates for migrants.

Essentially, the railroads were partners with the chambers of commerce in trying to promote the whole region (Ward 1994). The railroads were a necessary part of the tourism and migration priorities.

The only conflict within the recreation group was between the locals and tourism promoters. Tourists were not members of the forest community. They had a limited right to use the forest as it had been defined for them, and they had no management responsibilities. They were, however, a benefit stream in themselves and interference with that benefit stream by local recreationists was a problem. The problem surfaced with campgrounds built for tourists by the town commercial clubs. Local recreationists took all the choice spots early in the season, and set up camp for the whole season leaving little room for tourists (RCJ, 20 July 1919, p.1). There was a publicity campaign to inform the locals of their place in the world of resorts. The issue of local use in competition with tourist use came up from time to time, but before this simple common property period was over, recreational tourism was firmly established as a vital part of the Black Hills economy.

Miners as Part of the Community

Miners remained legitimate users of the forest since they had a legal right to mine on public land. They expanded the types of minerals they were looking for during this period. Mining companies were a far more important factor than individual prospectors. However, miners were really fringe members of the forest community because of their tunnel vision about the forest being simply a mining resource and their seeming lack of concern for the impact of mining on other uses of the forest.

The constant in mining was gold. Even though Homestake Mine dominated the gold industry, there were frequent, excited reports about gold strikes in the southern Hills, particularly around Hill City and Keystone. This period also included redevelopment of old gold strike sites for other minerals. For example, Leadville was developed first for gold, then lead and silver, and in 1910 for zinc carbonates (RCJ 26 January 1911, p.1).

Finding markets continued to be the biggest concern for minerals other than gold, and boom production followed when markets were developed for each. For example, mica mining boomed in Keystone Camp in June 1913 after an increase in demand for mica as a lubricant was reported in May 1913 (RCJ 10 June 1913, p.1 and 10 May 1913, p.1). An "inexhaustible" supply of pearl granite reported on February 4, 1914 had to wait for development because of a lack of markets (RCJ 4 February 1914, p.1). This period also included redevelopment of old gold strike sites for other minerals. Copper was developed starting in 1919 (RCJ 11 May 1919, p.1) and uranium was discovered at Keystone in 1918 (RCJ 24 December 1919, p.1), but there was no immediate market for it. Local capital became more of a factor in the development of mining than in the past.

Timber Users as Part of the Community

There were essentially two categories of timber users in this period: lumber companies, for commercial purposes, and local residents, for domestic purposes. The Forest Service timber priority was to take care of the needs of local residents and communities first, supply mines, and then if allowable cut was not exceeded, sell for general market (Newport 1956:34; Report of the Forester 1911).

Lumber company owners remained members of the forest community. The dean of lumber companies in the Black Hills at the time was Hinrichs Lumber Company. Its history is illustrative of the pattern of timber use by lumber companies. The company was formed in 1908 and was in continuous operation throughout this period, but underwent name changes to first become Lanphere Hinrichs and then Warren-Lamb (Hood 1928). The progress of this company was closely followed by the *Rapid City Journal* both in terms of its contribution to employment opportunities (RCJ 19 February 1913, p.1: 175 men employed) and its use of National Forest timber (RCJ 26 March 1913, p.1, 5/5/14, p.1: purchase contracts reported). The terms of the timber contracts illustrate the manner of doing business with the Forest Service. For example, a September 1913 contract called for the purchase of eleven million board feet of yellow pine over three years. The timber was for local consumption and the contract required removal of 70 percent of the merchantable timber during the contract and rights to make a second cut in twenty-thirty years (RCJ 30 September 13, p.1). A May 1914 contract called for the purchase of 153 million board feet of timber on a thirteen-year contract on twenty-seven thousand acres in the Spring Creek drainage area in both Harney and Black Hills National Forests. Lanphere Hinrichs had to construct twenty-five miles of railroad to get the timber to its Rapid City plant for processing and sale in and east of Rapid City. The article stressed that only mature timber was being taken and that it would actually improve the forest. Brush also had to be carefully taken care of so that it was not a fire hazard (RCJ 5 May 1914, p.1). Fig. 9 is an early lumber yard.

Warren-Lamb was a diversified lumber company, able to adjust its output to the market conditions (Warren 1928). This made it a stable member of the forest community. During a lumber slump other outfits closed, but Warren-Lamb kept going because it went into the market for grain doors and boxes (RCJ 19 September 1915, p.1). Considerable quantities of timber were also sold to Homestake and Burlington Railroad. A few large companies did the bulk of timber contracting, and many small operators accounted for a small proportion of the timber contracts. In 1914 there were 425 individual timber contracts in the Black Hills Forest Reserve and 417 for less than one hundred dollars. The long-term nature of the timber contracts attempted to promote a future orientation among commercial forest users that had been absent in the early days of the Black Hills forest use.

The domestic users of timber did not have the same contractual long-term interest as lumber companies, but they did have a clear interest in the continued existence of the forest. Domestic users were allowed to cut timber for building and maintaining their homesteads or mining activities and to collect dead and diseased timber for firewood or other domestic purposes. Using the dead and down timber was beneficial for the settlers because it provided firewood, and it was beneficial to forest management because it lessened the chance of forest fires. In 1915 there

Figure 9. Early Lumber Yard

were 147 sales to homesteaders and settlers and 1,255 free-use permits for dead and down timber to settlers and miners (RCJ 5 September 1915, p.1).

Ranchers and Stockmen as Part of the Community

Ranchers with holdings outside the Forest Reserve became members of the forest community during this period. These plains ranchers needed to graze their cattle in the forest in the summers. They were second in priority to forest residents for grazing permits and they took an active part in the management of the forest by tending the grazing lands and policing the area. In 1913 local ranchers formed an organization and sought to cooperate with the Forest Service to improve grazing conditions and to police the grazing (RCJ 7 September 1913, p.1). Increased grazing was supposed to bring about better utilization of the forest and increase revenues without placing a burden on individual permittees. Grazing applications increased in the latter stages of this period. Congress had authorized more homestead grants on prairies so stockmen had to turn to the national forests (RCJ 30 March 1917, p.1).

About once a year there was a newspaper article in the fall describing what a good grazing place the Black Hills was and how valuable the grazing resource was. The value of the grazing industry in BHNF in 1917 was reported at three million dollars (one and a half million

Figure 10. Replanting after a forest fire near Custer

dollars for cattle, half a million dollars for horses and a million dollars for ranch property owned by applicants). In 1919 the BHNF issued 500 grazing permits for 25,000 head of cattle; the largest permit went to W. D. Driskill of Spearfish for 3,500 head (RCJ 3 May 1919, p.1).

Commercial grazers were allowed into the forest community, as well. On June 15, 1913 the RCJ reported that a big Texas cattle company had brought sixteen hundred head of three- and four-year-old cattle to the BHNF for pasturage in the summer and fall. They paid $1.25 per head and planned to market the steers in Rapid City in the fall. There was no public outcry about "outsiders" using the grazing resources. There seemed to be plenty of grazing land to go around, except for sheep.

Exclusions from the Forest Community

In a common property resource scheme the group having ownership rights must be clearly defined. That definition is clarified by examining who is excluded from access to the resource. Although the earlier description of the forest community may seem inclusive, there were four distinctive groups who were excluded from access to the Black Hills National Forest in this time: 1) illegitimate miners; 2) sheep farmers; 3) the state of South Dakota; and 4) the Indians.

The example that demonstrates most clearly how the common property resource scheme worked during this time is the issue of sheep grazing. Sheep were barred in the Black Hills National Forest by Gifford Pinchot in 1909, but there were many sheep both on patented land within the forest and on neighboring land. Pinchot's reasoning was that the introduction would retard settlement of the country and the establishment of homes because they would destroy range upon which settlement was dependent. He also thought it would be dangerous to the development of the forest because the forest had so recently been ravaged by pine beetles that letting grazing sheep would threaten the new seedlings. Pinchot wanted to render all reasonable assistance to homebuilders and keeping sheep off the land would help (RCJ 25 August 1909). Pinchot held two meetings with the settlers, who were against allowing sheep by a margin of 3 to 1 (ibid.).

By 1911 sheep were a significant part of the agricultural economy of the region. Not all of the grazing permits for cattle and horses were applied for in 1911. A group of sheep farmers petitioned the Department of Agriculture to be allowed to use the remaining allocated permits for their sheep. According to the *Rapid City Journal,* the Forest

Service sent an official from Washington, D.C., to investigate their request. He met with cattlemen before his meeting with the sheep farmers and told the cattlemen they had better apply for all allocated grazing permits in the future. When he held a public meeting on the sheep farmers' request he took a vote of the settlers and the holders of stock (cattle and horses) grazing permits to see if the "forest community" wanted to expand to include sheep farmers. To no one's surprise they did not (RCJ 25 August 1909, p.1; 13 June 1911, p.1; 23 June 1911, p.1). By 1916, however, the community did decide to include sheep farmers, probably because the price of wool was up and the price of beef was down.

The State of South Dakota claimed title land in the National Forest because at the time of statehood, the federal government granted the sixteenth and thirty-sixth section of each township to the state to be used for educational purposes. A total of one hundred sections within the bounds of the Black Hills National Forest were theoretically state land under this grant. These "school lands" were generally set aside at the time of statehood. The Department of Interior had claimed that since no sections had been identified by survey at the time the National Forest was established, the state was not entitled to any land. The state argued that the school lands passed to state ownership whether surveyed or unsurveyed under the enabling act. The federal government finally gave in, but demanded that the state take ninety-five sections of land "in lieu of sections 16 and 36" near the border of the Reserve and that the border would be reestablished to exclude state lands in order to prevent state interference with administration of the Reserve (Green 1940:234). The ninety-five sections amounted to about two townships of land in the southeast corner of the Reserve that eventually became Custer State Park. The state's title was recognized by an agreement between the state and federal governments on January 4, 1910. Five other sections within the Forest's boundaries had been surveyed by the time of the agreement, adding to the state's total (Green at 234). During this first common property resource period, state officials were kept out of forest management decisions by the segregation of state land.

Exclusion of the Sioux Indians seemed very much in the public consciousness. Public notice of the exclusion of the Sioux was the result of reports of Sioux efforts to regain the Hills and fruitless efforts by some whites to have memorials in the Hills to the Indians. It was suggested in 1910 that there should be Indian memorials in Dark Canyon because that had been a favorite Indian spot. The reasoning was:

Before invasion by white men the Black Hills were a favorite resort for the Indians and cherished by them as a favorite hunting ground. Since being excluded from the Hills the Indians have continued to look with covetous eyes on their lost possession. (RCJ 20 April 1910, p.1).

This kind of Indian sympathizing brought forward historian Doane Robinson who wrote a letter to the editor of the *Rapid City Journal* entitled "The Truth About the Hills Treaty." The thrust of the letter was that the government acted in good faith and the Indians had nothing to complain about (RCJ 22 April 1910, p.1). In 1912 the Wannamakers, an industrial family, tried to get the government to set aside a section in the Hills as a camping place for the Indians and have it located near where Indian memorials would be carved or erected (RCJ 12 March 1912, p.1). This request fell on deaf ears.

There was not great resistance to the excluding the above-mentioned groups from access to the benefits of the Black Hills National Forest during this period. The forest community was stable and able to take in new members of the clearly defined group without taxing the resource. It was during this period, in 1908, that Congress passed legislation sharing 25 percent of National Forest receipts with the counties in which the Forests were located. The financial contribution to the local communities could be interpreted as recognition that the Forests were, in fact, part of the communities and should make a contribution to maintain the communities. The shared revenue was used for schools and roads. This shared revenue also recognized the Forest as an economic asset of the communities from which they should reap a benefit. The way in which the forest community managed the forest in conjunction with the Forest Service will show that all of the elements of a common property scheme were present in this period.

The Sustainable Management Scheme

The last test of a common property management scheme is a sustainable management plan, adhered to by the ownership group. The question to be answered in this case is whether management of the forest was entirely in the hands of the government or whether the forest community identified above had substantial management rights and responsibilities. The management plan during this period had two major components: regulations initiated by the Forest Service and by the local forest community. Timber and grazing were most heavily regulated by the Forest Service, but even in those areas there was substantial local input into the regulations and local participation in their enforcement. For example, grazing capacity was established jointly by the Forest Service and the stockmen, and monitoring of adherence to the grazing regulations was done primarily by the stockmen's association (RCJ 30 March 1917, p.1). This arrangement of public and private participation is very similar to the kind of institution Ostrom (1991) noticed in many of the successful common property resource schemes she examined.

Because of the history of timber pillaging in the Black Hills, the general public and the forest community both needed to be taught that timber was a crop to be tended instead of mined. Due to the previous timber cutting, particularly in the Northern Hills, there was great concern that there would be a timber shortage that would hurt the mining industry. So at the insistence of the mining industry, there was a ban on selling forest reserve timber to out-of-state consumers that was not lifted until 1912 (Duthie 1928:105).

Newport (1956) describes this period from 1905 to 1920 as the "Technical Forestry Takes Over Period" because of the implementation of scientific forestry under the Department of Agriculture. The Black Hills National Forest was chosen as a place to demonstrate scientific forestry methods because the lumber industry was dependent on the Forest Reserve and the success or failure of new methods would be evident.

Two principles of scientific forestry were important in this period. The first was the concept of allowable cut based on the reproductive capacity of the forest. The second was to turn the Black Hills National Forest into a monoculture of yellow ponderosa pine. Between 1905 and 1912 it became evident that there would be a continuous supply of timber for the foreseeable future if only as much timber was cut as could regenerate in a year. This amount became known as the allowable cut. It was not until well after this first common property period that timber harvest even approached the allowable cut because of the lack of market pressures. The regulations applied to timber harvests were aimed at sustainable yield. They were necessary because of the tragedy of the commons that had occurred so recently during the open-access period. The long-term nature of the timber contracts was intended to give lumber companies a stake in future growth as well as to better manage current harvests.

Pinchot's forest management philosophy required that management questions be decided based on the local economy, with the needs of the dominant local industries being paramount (Newport 1956:29; Pinchot

1947). In 1907 forestry experts from the Yale School of Forestry suggested that all reseeding in the Black Hills be confined to ponderosa Pine because it had the greatest marketability of all species that could survive in the Black Hills climate (RCJ 20 July 1907, p.1). In the Black Hills both mining and lumbering were dominant industries. During this period there were enough forest resources to meet the needs of both industries, so there was no conflict.

There also needed to be some policing of timber use by homesteaders because not all homesteaders adhered to the sustained use management plan. Policing was done both by the government officials and other homesteaders or summer residents. Apparently some of the homesteaders were speculating in timber and selling all that they could cut from their homesteads. The Forest Service announced restrictions on homesteaders cutting timber in the reserve in April 1914. They could cut timber from the area to be cultivated, for building fences, and other improvements and they could sell a surplus timber from the cultivated area. However, they could not denude the plot to sell it as agricultural land or speculate on land before title passed. They could not cut timber for sale, no matter how the money was to be used. If the settlement claim was abandoned after timber was cut, there was a presumption that the primary purpose of the claim was for timber. Dead or diseased timber came under a different set of rules (RCJ 7 April 1914, p.6).

Grazing was the other area that needed government authority behind the regulations, although there was substantial local input. When ranchers were brought into the forest community, they formed a local organization and cooperated with the forest service to solve mutual problems. One thing the Forest Service and the stockowners association worked on was increasing the number of animals that could be grazed on forest range. The grazing capacity increased because of improved methods of handling animals and new watering places opened new areas to grazing. During this period there were no reports of degradation of the Hills' grazing lands. It appeared that the carrying capacity of the land was not exceeded until after this period had come to a close. When sheep were finally allowed to graze on the Forest, the stockmen's association helped work out the formula of one cow being equal to five sheep in grazing units (RCJ 7 September 1913, p.1). One thing absent from the discussions about managing grazing activities was mention of grazers poaching on the forest by putting more animals out to pasture than the permits allowed. This absence does not mean that there were no poachers, only that it was not perceived as a big problem during this period.

Recreationists assumed management responsibilities in several ways. Local sportsmen and recreation promoters put considerable effort into turning the Black Hills into a trout fishing area. Trout are not native to the Black Hills, but were introduced to the Hills by a Rapid City businessman in 1888 and they became the favorite sport fish. Trout are a fairly delicate fish and will not breed under the conditions in the Black Hills so they needed to be stocked annually. Local sportsmen's clubs and railroad companies did most of the stocking, although the Forest Service also participated. (RCJ 2 October 10, p.1; 22 March 1911, p.1). The Chicago, Black Hills, and Western Railroad stocked Rapid Creek with 10 million trout from the Spearfish Hatchery (RCJ 17 April 1913. p. 5). The various railroads serving the Hills promoted the Black Hills as a trout fisherman's paradise at the time. Black Hills sportsmen not only stocked trout but they also planted celery, watercress, moss, and grass along streams as trout food (RCJ 1 February 1912, p. 2). Trout are also very sensitive to water pollution and because of the trout tourism business, there was considerable pressure to keep *some* of the streams relatively pollution-free. The accommodation between the polluters (mostly miners) and recreationists resulted in some streams being informally designated as pollution-free zones for trout (Spearfish Creek) while others remained public sewers (Whitewood Creek). One of the few evidences of tension about forest use at this time could be inferred from an article on the importance of summer tourists in boosting the Black Hills and what a big mistake it was to allow pollution of Rapid Creek waters (RCJ 26 September 1911, p.5). Even this tension was very mild, however.

In addition to ensuring the presence of the recreational resource, the recreationists took control over its management by organizing to enforce game laws. In 1911 fish and game clubs formed in the Northern Hills to stock streams and enforce game laws (RCJ 22 March 1911, p.1). The Black Hills Game Protective Association was formed to see that game laws were enforced to stop the wholesale slaughter of deer.

Building a forest community seemed to have positive effects. The Forest Service announced a successful fire season in 1914. In the past settlers had been a major cause of fires, but now the people living in the forest deserved credit for not letting them start, or putting them out quickly (RCJ 17 December 1914, p.1). Fire control had been one of the management functions that the Forest Service designated in order to obtain the help of the forest community.

There were limits to how much the forest community could assert control over changing forest management because of the need for Forest Service cooperation. Jewel Cave is an example of the negotiation process between the community and the Forest Service. Jewel Cave is located west of Custer in the southern part of the Black Hills National Forest. During this time the cave was believed to contain about eight hundred rooms in its forty miles of passages (Schrader 1909) although more rooms were discovered later. The Michaud brothers had staked a mining claim in 1900, and for about four months a year for three years they worked the cave as a jasper and manganese claim. After they had spent several hundred dollars and never found marketable quantities of either mineral, they thought about using the cave as a tourist attraction and started charging a modest fee for people to go through the cave.

Using the cave as a tourist attraction was a substantial definitional change and such private enterprise was outside the definition of acceptable uses according to the forest community. The Michaud brothers seemed unconcerned with the technical illegality of their proposed use. The local community was not opposed to using the cave as a tourist attraction, but wanted it set aside as a national monument. Some people also suggested that the government establish a sixty-square-mile game preserve with the cave as the centerpoint. The Forest Service investigated and recommended against a game preserve because the animals were not unique (they could be found in Yellowstone National Park), but did recommend setting aside approximately 1,280 acres as a national monument, which was done on February 7, 1908.

The forest community wanted more than national monument status, however. They expected there to be some protection of the cave from mining activity and some development of it as a natural wonder. There were no federal funds appropriated for such development and the Michauds' mining claims were not invalidated by the new status of the cave. Even though the Michauds were more interested in tourism than mining, some of their claims were found valid by investigators so their ownership was still intact (Report of Expert Miner, H. M. Booth on Jewel et al., 22 July 1911). From the establishment of the national monument in 1908 until 1919 the government took no action with regard to Jewel Cave other than to investigate the Michaud mining claims. From Michaud's correspondence with the Forest Service during this time it appeared that he really wanted the government to buy his mining claims, and when they took no action or showed no interest, he sold calcite from the cave to get some return on his investment and get the government's attention. Members of the forest community complained loudly to the Forest Service every time minerals were removed from the cave. The cave had been advertised in tourism brochures since 1908, but when people would reach it, they would be unable to enter.

The Forest Service Supervisor decided to start some action in 1919 by writing to the District Forester in Denver and requesting a final decision on ownership of the cave. It had been practically closed to the public since 1908, although the Forest Supervisor considered it an important factor in increasing the attractiveness of the Forest for recreation (Letter 9 May 1919 U.S. Forest Service, Custer S. D.). The District Forester requested action by the Solicitor General because the cave was being exploited as a natural curiosity, not as a mining claim. On July 7, 1919, Assistant Forester Stahl recommended to the Supervisor of Harney Forest (the southern portion of the present Black Hills National Forest) that the executive order creating Jewel Cave National Monument be revoked because the cave was not unusual in the Black Hills and was not very attractive or interesting, in addition to being dangerous in its present state (Stahl Report, 7 July 1919 U.S. Forest Service, Custer, S.D.). Obviously that recommendation would not have been popular with the forest community and there was no indication that it was ever made public. In a way the forest community and the Forest Service were at an impasse with the Michauds owning the mining claims and wanting development for tourism purposes and the government being without resources to develop the cave. (See letter from Stahl to Michaud, 6 January 1920, U.S. Forest Service, Custer, S.D.) Pressure was put on the Forest Service in many ways. The Commercial Club continued to advertise Jewel Cave and asked Senator Peter Norbeck to request appropriations to buy out the Michaud claim (November 1923 letter from Commercial Club to Norbeck, U.S. Forest Service, Custer, S.D.). Part of the urgency for buying out the claim was that the cave was unsafe for visitors in its present condition. The only result was that the Forest Service padlocked the cave to prevent vandalism and injury. It was not until 1965 that the National Park Service took over development responsibilities to make Jewel Cave accessible to the public for recreational purposes (Memorandum of Understanding Between the United States Forest Service Department of Agriculture and the National Park Service, Department of the Interior, February 9, 1965).

The Black Hills National Forest and the economic resources contained in it were major factors in the development of a transportation infrastructure to western South Dakota and eastern Wyoming. The infrastructure was essential to the survival of the forest community. From 1910 to 1913 development of coal resources in Wyoming brought extensions of the Black Hills and Western Railroad and McLaughlin lines (RCJ 27 February 1910, p.1; 23 May 1913, p.1). However, the rate structure could not favor development of rail service to the Black Hills because of the relatively small amount of freight compared to the long distance it must be hauled. Railroads were continually being asked to establish special rates for the Black Hills. For example, in 1914 the South Dakota Railroad Commission ordered a reduction of 35 percent in rates for lumber products coming out of the Black Hills (RCJ 2 May 1914, p.1) and the mayor of Rapid City asked for special homeseekers rates (RCJ 23 July 1914, p.1). The railroads, which had played such a big factor in the initial development of the Black Hills, started to lose their economic viability in this period.

Roads were an integral part of both the management of the National Forest and the development of the region and forest community. The Black Hills played a prominent role in getting approval for a highway to connect western South Dakota with the eastern part of the country. Tourism was the theme that justified the construction of the first road, the Black and Yellow Trail, which extended from Chicago to Yellowstone through the Black Hills. The picture painted was of tourists lined up at the other end of roads being built from Iowa and Nebraska, just waiting for the roads to open so they could rush to see the Black Hills (RCJ 10 September 1913, p.1). The trail was promoted enthusiastically by boosters throughout the Hills, and although tourism was the thrust of the promotion, the road was expected to be a major factor in the development of the West (RCJ 16 September 1913, p.1). The National Highway Association designated the Black and Yellow Trail an official tour route in 1914 (RCJ 20 August 1914, p.1). Most of the commercial boosting was about the value of the Black Hills as a resort. The emphasis in construction was on scenic highways, not necessarily the shortest route between two points. Good roads were particularly important because tourists coming into the area from the eastern United

States were suing the counties for damage to their cars caused by poor roads (RCJ 24 June 1913, p.1).

Intra-Hills highways and roads were at least as important as the outside connections. None of these roads could be built without being a part of the Forest Reserve, and the burden for financing these roads lay with the Forest Service through timber contracts and grazing fees. Congress also specifically appropriated money for forest roads for the benefit of settlers and communities beyond main highways. It was the Forest Service's intention to set the standard for communities in road building (RCJ 5 May 1914, p.1). In 1919 the federal government spent $1,250,000 on forest roads, with $93,000 going to Black Hills and Harney Forests to improve a main highway between Deadwood and Hot Springs (RCJ 6 April 1919, p.1). The role of the forest community in the roads issue was demonstrated by meetings called to endorse better roads in the Black Hills. An example was the meeting called by the Black Hills Stockgrowers who endorsed better roads from Custer to Hill City (all within National Forest bounds) to help establish a cash market in Custer (RCJ 31 July 1915, p.1).

Summary of the Period

In this first simple common property period, a forest community was successfully established. The National Forest was an integral part of the Black Hills community. The multiple-use resource definition advocated by Gifford Pinchot was implemented through the construction of the forest community. The Forest Service played a major, but not exclusive role in monitoring use and maintenance of the resource elements in the Forest. Timber demand was easily met under the allowable cut standards that promoted sustainability. Through timber contracts lumber companies gained long-term interests in the forest and had forest maintenance responsibilities that they willingly accepted. Grazing regulations were adopted only after consultation with the stockmen's associations, which also took on range-management duties. Recreationists nurtured the trout industry. The Black Hills were not a pristine environment during this period; mining still openly polluted streams, but there was a conscious effort to maintain a multiple-use environment.

Within the accepted uses, the definitions were fairly narrow, but they also changed over time. Sheep first were excluded, then included when attitudes changed. Recreation expanded from hunting and fishing to include scenic highways. It was also during this time that the Black Hills

National Forest began the process of becoming a ponderosa pine mono-culture when reseeding efforts were intentionally restricted because pine had the best market potential of any species that would grow in the region.

Many seeds for later conflicts were planted during this period, con-flicts over exclusion from the forest community and over the definition of a multiple-use resource, as well as conflicts about the place of roads in national forests. However, for the forest community of this period, the resource was well defined, the community boundaries were clear, and a management plan was developed by all community members.

Chapter 4

Dissolution of the Common Property Scheme

One of the beauties of a common property resource (CPR) management scheme is that it can function in perpetuity. Common property resources such as grazing lands (Orlove 1976; Sheridan 1988), lobsters (Acheson 1988), coastal fisheries (Pinkerton 1987) and irrigation systems (Ostrom 1991) have continued to form the basis of local economies for generations. In all of those cases the resource remained clearly defined, the group entitled to exploit it was cohesive, and the use was maintained by the user community at a sustainable level. Until 1919 the forest community was really a group of multiple users as well as users of a multiple-use resource. Farmers cut timber, almost everyone mined a little, and there was a feeling of responsibility within the forest community for what went on in the National Forest. Changes had been made in the definition of the multiple uses, and of emphasis which use had the greatest importance had changed, but these decisions were handled within the forest community. The Black Hills National Forest had the potential to continue to function as a stable, multiple-use common property resource.

This chapter examines how the common property resource scheme unraveled and what some of the ramifications were. Each element of the CPR framework changed. The definition of the Forest as a resource changed from multiple use to many uses, even though the same category of uses remained under the statute. The forest community was split into users of individual parts and the forest community was no longer treated like owners. Once again the government took on the role of owner and made management decisions without consulting the forest community. Overall there was a qualitative change away from building

79

a forest community that would sustain the forest to using the forest to support economic goals. The change in emphasis from forest community to a larger economic community made a substantial difference in both how people related to the forest as a resource and how they related to each other as members of the forest community.

Three distinctive resource definition periods are involved in this "non common property period" which began about 1920 and ended in the mid-1960s. The first of the three periods, from 1920 to 1932, was the era of change in management practices. The overriding theme was zoning of the forest, meaning that the multiple-use definition was altered from many uses of the whole to many specific uses of specific sections of the forest: wildlife areas, working circles for timber harvesting, recreation areas, and others. The expressed goal was to make the forest community (now meaning the towns in the Forest) more economically stable. One of the concerns in western South Dakota was population loss during this time. People moved away from the Black Hills to cities in the Midwest where the jobs were when the United States entered World War I. Between 1910 and 1920 the Black Hills counties lost almost 18 percent of their population.

The second period of resource redefinition was a time when fundamental changes were made to the resources in the Black Hills National Forest while still staying within the original categories of protection of watershed, timber, recreation, grazing land, and mining. From 1933 to World War II the New Deal had a great impact on the Forest. The New Deal's public works projects substantially added to the resource elements in the forest. During this time the infrastructure of the forest was maintained by public service programs. The third portion of this period, 1946 to the mid-1960s, was a time for entrepreneurial opportunism in exploiting the Forest both as a whole and for its individual aspects. There was an intentional and aggressive effort to visualize the forest resources as private economic development tools. Public works programs were no longer available to maintain the infrastructure. Together, these three periods were times of conflict among user groups, times when lines were drawn over issues of control, with the Forest Service usually being the decision maker. The population decline reversed to a trend of modest gains, but most the gains were in established towns, particularly in urban Pennington County, which between 1920 and 1960 grew from 12,720 people to 58,185 people. The users of the forest were no longer serving as managers, so not only did they not make management decisions, they also did not take on management responsibilities.

The greatest changes in the resource definition came with the literal addition of resources to the forest: reservoirs, lakes, wildlife preserves, and the monuments Mount Rushmore and Crazy Horse. Even those additions fit within the established multiple-use categories of timber, grazing, recreation, mining, and watershed protection. Rather than providing a chronological account of the Forest's history, this chapter analyses how the resource definition changed and what became of the concept of forest community that led to the breakdown of the sustainable management plan and degradation of the Black Hills National Forest as a multiple-use resource. (Each sector of the former forest community is discussed separately.)

The Role of the Timber Sector

Between 1920 and the mid-1960s, timber management made a profound contribution to the change in the overall resource definition and the composition of the forest community. Timber had always been central to the resource definition of the forest, and during the previous common property period all members of the forest community shared timber-cutting privileges to some degree. Use by the forest community had not threatened the integrity of the forest in any way, but it had spawned myriad small, competing sawmills throughout the Hills (Linde 1984). During the economic depression of the late 1920s and early 1930s, many small, portable sawmills were operated by Black Hills residents in need of cash (Newport 1956). Almost all of the timber was used locally. Timber of the quality grown in the Black Hills was not in great demand outside the Hills, but it serviced the needs of the Black Hills region quite well.

First through the working circle concept, and later through the sustained yield unit management concept, the group entitled to the timber benefit stream narrowed considerably, thereby altering the forest community and unraveling the sustainable management plan. It is somewhat ironic that the timber management plans would play so prominent a role in the breakdown of the common property scheme and degradation of the forest as a whole, when the timber resource itself did not suffer any significant damage and in fact, flourished in this period.

The working circle concept of National Forest management was implemented in the Black Hills National Forest as a pilot project in the early 1920s. The entire forest was divided into nine working circles based on watersheds for the purpose of establishing timber-cutting budgets for ponderosa pine and white spruce, administering timber

contracts, and most, importantly, fostering the development of permanent marketing centers throughout the Black Hills (Duthie 1922). The
prevailing attitude about the national forest timber supply was that with
scientific management, treating timber as a crop, not a mine, meant the
Black Hills timber was inexhaustible (Duthie 1928:101). In the early
1920s the questions of allowable cut and by whom timber could be cut
were answered through the working circle management plans. Part of
the working circle plan was to offer timber contracts to mill-owning
customers only, not to contractors or middlemen (Newport 1956:45).
The reasons were outlined by Forest Supervisor George Duthie in 1922
as follows:

> Where enough stumpage is tributary to a central marketing point to as-
> sure an operation long enough to depreciate the investment, it is reason-
> able to suppose that permanent types of mills, fully equipped to manu-
> facture lumber economically and well, will supplant the inefficient and
> wasteful portable mill now so commonly used. Permanent mills of this
> kind will not only reduce waste in manufacture but they will result in
> broader, more stable markets and a closer utilization in the woods. The
> other advantages of better labor and housing conditions, the reduction of
> fire hazard and of the unsightly camps from the elimination of the
> portable sawmill camp are added reasons why we should shape our sales
> policies to bring about the establishment of a permanent logging and
> marketing center for each working circle. Pursuant to this policy it shall
> be the policy to discourage any more new operators from becoming es-
> tablished on the Forests. There are now 55 mills within or adjacent to the
> boundaries of the Black Hills and Harney Forests which depend upon the
> National Forests for all or part of their timber. . . . It is therefore a sound
> economic policy to discourage the establishment of any more portable
> mills with their poor equipment and inefficient methods and encourage
> the establishment of a permanent type of about 20 M(illion) board feet
> daily capacity at sites where the investment in permanent equipment can
> be amply depreciated. (Duthie 922:16,17)

The damage to the common property resource scheme came from the
withdrawal of timber from the reach of the broad forest community. An
alliance was forged between the Forest Service and established timber
operators. Timber became the property of the Forest Service to dispose
of as it saw fit. The working circle's goal of efficiency in timber use
gave way to one of promoting community stabilization during the Great
Depression. Policies that the Forest Service thought would stabilize the
community actually very destructive of the forest community established during the prior period.

For the established lumber companies that the Forest Service chose to support, the policy was very advantageous. For instance, the timber in the Nemo working circle was unofficially reserved for the Homestake Mining Company of Lead and Deadwood (ibid.). Warren-Lamb Lumber Company of Rapid City was kept afloat by this preferential policy as well as lower stumpage rates (Newport 1956:47). (Stumpage rates are a method of charging by reviewing the stumps rather than measuring the board feet of processed lumber.) Warren-Lamb was the showpiece of the Black Hills timber operators because of its efficient harvesting, production, and marketing methods (RCJ 8 May 1920; Laughlin 1940). The policy of sustaining Warren-Lamb caused problems with small mill operators who were being forced out of business. In June 1936 the Forest Service began to reserve some small cuts for small operators. One aspect of allowing small operators to obtain timber permits was an arrangement for them to sell to Warren-Lamb and have Warren-Lamb do the marketing (Newport at 53, 56). The Forest Service clearly liked the way working circles operated. The management plan for the Custer Working Circle was published by the Department of Agriculture as a model for other forests to follow (Webster 1928).

As if the working circles did not limit timber access enough, the Sustained Yield Act of 1944 made it possible to reduce or eliminate competition under some circumstances. In 1947 the Forest Service toyed with the idea of setting up a Custer Federal Sustained Yield Unit, setting aside the Custer working circle for the exclusive use of the wood-using industries in Custer, Hill City, and Pringle and virtually eliminating competition from the outside in order to gain stability in the local community industry and also to improve the use of the timber. However, local citizens had to accept a Sustained Yield Unit. The Forest Service perceived there was opposition to it in Custer, so it was never presented to the town (Newport at 77). Homestake did operate within a Sustained Yield Unit even though there was some local dissatisfaction with the dominance of Homestake over the resources of the northern Black Hills National Forest (Newport at 78). One of the conclusions reached by Newport was that monopoly use resulted in much better utilization of the forest resources than competitive use did (Newport at 86).

The Forest Service controlled the amount of timber that could be cut, guided by the mandate that national forests were not to be deforested. Allowable cut for the Black Hills National Forest was more of an issue between the Forest Service and South Dakota than between the Forest

Service and timber operators. South Dakota complained that the National Forest was being undercut and that private forests were being over-cut (Ware 1936). State legislators thought it was important for South Dakota, a prairie state, to be self-sufficient in timber even though the self-sufficiency would be short-lived and the resources depleted. Although it remained a source of contention, the Forest Service did not change its "allowable cut" policy in response to state demands.

A sustainable management plan, even just for timber, not for the entire multiple-use resource, had to include maintenance of the stock. During this period, public works programs, not the forest community, performed the maintenance tasks of thinning stands of trees, planting, improving water availability, insect control, and building a transportation infrastructure for fire control (RCJ 2 May 1933, p.1; Alleger 1935; RCJ 28 July 1941, p.7). The thinning done by the Civilian Conservation Corps (CCC) was the only thinning program that had been carried out in the forest since its creation. Thinning the forest released the trees for growth at three or four times their previous growth rate (Newport 1956). Thinning the trees eliminated the "doghair stands" that presented a fire risk. See Fig. 10 in which men are replanting trees after a forest fire. The lack of forest community participation in maintaining the timber resource was a serious departure from the common property scheme. Before this period the gathering of firewood and cutting for fence posts had at least partially fulfilled the thinning chore.

By the early 1960s an adversarial relationship developed between timber operators and the Forest Service over stumpage prices. In addition to complaining about the price, timber operators complained about the process of setting the price, which they felt was arbitrary (RCJ 25 January 1961, p.3). A more telling complaint about the state of the forest community was that they felt the Forest Service employees were not properly trained for work in the Black Hills and that they did not stay around long enough to get acquainted (RCJ 15 March 1961, p.3). Such a situation was a marked change from the policies of Gifford Pinchot and Seth Bullock in hiring local people and having the Forest Service be considered part of the forest community, not the boss of forest users. An outcome of the stumpage price confrontation was a government and industry study of five hundred pines from harvest through the board stage to see if the pricing system was fair. Aside from the economic ramifications of the study, both groups changed their attitudes about each other as the work went on (RCJ 24 April 1962, p. 2). As a result of the study, the parties agreed on a stumpage price, with all parties knowing what it was based on. The community relations aspect of the pine study was probably more important than any change in stumpage rates.

A serious problem with making timber from the National Forest a cornerstone of the Black Hills economy in the early 1960s was that markets for Black Hills wood products were very hard to create. Simply supplying the local mining, railroad, and building needs was not enough to support communities with timber processing. The quality of Black Hills timber was another problem. In the twelve-state pine region 33.83 percent of a log could be realized, while in the Black Hills this proportion was only 5.4 percent (RCJ 27 June 1961, p. 2). This difference was the result of the short growing seasons in the Black Hills and the long growing cycle necessary to get a marketable tree. There was an excess of roundwood, small diameter timber that needed to be removed from the forest but was difficult to market. The failure to thin the forest was one cause of the excess of roundwood.

In the mid-1950s, there had been considerable attention paid to the idea of setting up a pulp mill in the Black Hills to process this roundwood. When the Forest Service Research Center was established in Rapid City in 1955, pulpwood prospects were the first item on the agenda. The center was looking for a use for the small timber because its over presence reduced the amount of forage for cattle, sheep, and wildlife, and used too much scarce water (RCJ 10 July 1955, p. 12). By October 1955 a pulpwood plant was in the blueprint stage (RCJ 5 October 1955, p. 12). The state Forestry Council pushed hard for a mill (RCJ 18 December 1956 p. 2), but there simply was not enough water available in the Black Hills to sustain the operation according to studies of the proposal (Chicago and NorthWestern Railway System 1955, 1956). Pulpwood did get utilized, but not in the Black Hills. It was shipped to Wisconsin and Iowa under very favorable rail rates (Chicago and NorthWestern Railway System 1956, 1964; RCJ 16 October 1960, p. 22). Products that could be made with inferior wood included chip board, particle board, lathes, bedding, mulching, stock feed, combination with chemicals for nylon, rayon for tires, and grain alcohol (RCJ 30 March 1958, p.8; RCJ 23 February 1960, p. 3).

The change in the resource definition of timber was dramatic. During the 1920 to mid-1960s time frame it had changed from a supportive role in relation to other uses of the National Forest, such as mining, firewood, and railroad ties, to an economic resource that was supposed to be profitable in its own right. In the process, timber operators were selected out of, or removed from, the forest community by the Forest Service and were given a direct relationship with the Forest Service as purchasers of timber, not as users and managers of the National Forest.

The Role of the Grazing Sector

Even though grazing remained an important element in the multiple use definition of the Forest, and the priorities for granting grazing permits remained the same from 1920 to the mid-1960s, the role of stockmen underwent several changes. Initially they were the core of the forest community, then they were the pariahs responsible for almost all environmental problems, and finally they became rehabilitated members of the forest community. The process by which this happened demonstrates how a breakdown in the forest community had significant ramifications for the condition of the forest as a multiple-use resource.

Early in this period sheep and cattle grazing within the National Forest was touted as a major use and a benefit to both the forest and the local community (Duthie 1928; Palais 1942). In the early 1920s there was an effort to stabilize the local agricultural economy by changing five-year grazing permits to ten-year permits with preferences going to permittees owning ranch property heavily dependent on grazing permits (RCJ 19 June 1923, p. 2). The new ten-year permits started in 1925 and made it easier to secure financing for raising stock based on the long-term interest in the grazing land. At that time, there seemed to be no shortage of grazing land. In fact, there was a major effort to increase the number of dairy farms around Custer, adding to the potential permittees (RCJ 27 August 1926, p.1).

Sometime in the 1930s, exactly when is impossible to determine, the carrying capacity for grazing land in the Black Hills National Forest was reached. The Forest Service started to reject almost as many applicants as they accepted for permits (See RCJ 2 March 1934, p. 1). Most of the rejected applications were from new applicants, so permittees seeking renewals felt secure about their vested grazing rights and their place in the forest community. The vested stockmen did not perceive a carrying capacity problem. They not only wanted longer permits, they wanted more permits, and they wanted to pay a lower fee tied to average beef and mutton prices. By the early 1940s some of the range land within the Forest was being severely overgrazed. Gullies started to form because of the lack of soil cover, and grasses were replaced by weeds. See Figure 11 which depicts gullying in the grazing areas of the Bear Lodge District. The Forest Service decided that the only way to protect and restore the grazing land was to reduce the number of grazing permits, not just turn down new permit requests.

Figure 11. Gullying in Bear Lodge District

An adversarial relationship started to develop between stockmen and the Forest Service. Reducing the number of permits was within the statutory authority of the Forest Service, and while the Forest Service legally implemented a reduction plan, but they did it unilaterally. The critical element was not necessarily the reduction of grazing permits but the deviation from the common property management scheme that would have made reductions a forest community decision.

Once ousted from the inner circle of the forest community, the stockmen adapted quickly to their new role as adversaries. In 1945 stockmen complained to Representative Case, their congressman, that the Forest Service was being unreasonable by limiting the number of grazing permits. Stockmen all over the West were complaining about the same thing and Congress asked the Forest Service to start a two-year study of the grazing situation (RCJ 10 October 1945, p. 2). Local complaints centered not on regulation by the Forest Service, but on the manner of regulation. After asserting that the stockmen did not oppose regulation of grazing, the stockmen's representative said:

> But the stockmen do oppose Forest Service administration that is frequently dictatorial, and as often stupid; that ignores everyday common sense and experience in land management. Cattle and sheep permits have steadily decreased according to stockmen since 1918. The Forest Service is unreasonable in wanting 50 to 70% of the forage on the ground at the end of the season to "revegetate." (RCJ 11 October 1948, p. 5).

The adversarial relationship was formally recognized with the formation of a local "impartial appeals board" representing public grazing permittees and the Forest Service at the direction of the House Public Lands Subcommittee (RCJ 22 October 1947, p. 1). The adversarial nature of the relationship crystallized with the formation of the Black Hills Association of Forest Users by stockmen in 1949. As a result of the political power of this organization, the number of permits increased rather than decreased in the late 1940s.

When the Forest Service again cancelled some temporary permits in 1950 to prevent (in the Forest Service's opinion) further damage to the grazing land, the Black Hills Association of Forest Users complained to the county commissioners that the Forest Service was devaluing their property by cutting back on permits and that there was no reason for the cutback because the Hills were not overgrazed. Out of this controversy, a Forest Advisory Board was established, which was composed of five members (selected by the Forest Service) representing city water, mining, sports, cattle, and sheep interests. The Forest Advisory Board examined a contested area in the Limestone District in Wyoming where the Forest Service wanted to reduce the permits by 60 percent and reported the following conditions. The cattle had eaten all the grass off the range, then browsed off the growth of willows, chokecherries, and all of the young quaking aspen. Only heavy growth was left for deer in the winter. There was no chance of reforesting the deciduous trees, and the cattle had eaten the leaves so high that all the deer might starve. The grass had been thinned so much that weeds had begun to grow (RCJ 29 September 1950, p. 12). However, the Forest Advisory Council was not unsympathetic to the grazing-permit holders and suggested that grasshoppers might have caused some of the damage. They advised the Forest Service to make reductions only where necessary and restore the permits if and when improvements of the range allowed it. Permit cuts were to be implemented over two to three years (RCJ 5 October 1950, p. 3).

The grazing issue was not just about cattle- and sheep-grazing range. It was actually a conflict within the multiple use definition, because not only cattle and sheep grazed on the land, but deer also depended on forage in the forest. Cattle and sheep only grazed during the summer, while deer depended on forest vegetation all year round. As might have been expected, when the grazing situation reached a point where there was not enough forage for both deer and the permitted cattle and sheep, a feud developed between sportsmen and the Black Hills ranchers over the grazing problem. The feud was aggravated by a multiple-jurisdiction problem. The Forest Service had jurisdiction over the sheep and cattle, but the wild animals were under the jurisdiction of the state governments of South Dakota and Wyoming.

In October 1950 the Black Hills Rod and Gun Club passed a resolution supporting the Forest Service's reduction of grazing by 60 percent. At the club meeting a South Dakota Game Warden showed pictures of how sheep and cattle were destroying grazing land. After the passage of the resolution, eighty ranchers in Fall River County issued public notice that they would allow no hunting or trespassing on land except by special permission and that all members of the Black Hills Rod and Gun Club would be refused permission on any and all land owned or controlled by ranchers (RCJ 20 October 1950, p. 1).

The grazing permit cuts started in 1951, with the Black Hills Association of Forest Users fighting them at every turn. They brought in experts from the University of Wyoming who said grasshoppers were the problem. They complained that the grazing cut would decrease tax revenue (RCJ 20 February 1951, p. 10). The Black Hills Farm and Ranch Institute held a forum defending the stockmen, telling people that ranchers were responsible and knew when grass was being overgrazed. They portrayed the ranchers as small farmers (the average permittee on the Black Hills owned thirty-six head while the national average was sixty-three) and as conservationists. Additionally they said the grazing capacity of western South Dakota was actually unknown. The stockmen said that overgrazers were a minority and that grasshoppers and porcupines were hurting the grasslands (RCJ 25 February 1951, p. 1).

In 1954 the condition of the grazing land was blamed for the Black Hills water shortage even though there had been a cumulative water deficit since 1950, according to researchers at the Black Hills Research Center. The Rapid City chapter of the Izaak Walton League, a conservation groups of sportsmen, determined (to their own satisfaction) that the dwindling water supply was caused by overgrazing and that streams were even drying up because of grazing problems. The Walton League warned that there would not be any water in the Hills if the overgrazing was not stopped (RCJ 18 October 1954, p. 3). Other sports groups also blamed the stockmen for wildlife browse problems:

> Tempers flared over controversial stock grazing at Black Hills Rod and Gun Club. Following arguments by ranchers and stockmen, a resolution passed backing contentions in the *Sioux Falls-Argus Leader* newspaper that over-grazing by stock in the Black Hills is seriously endangering the recreational areas, wildlife and watershed. (RCJ 7 October 1954, p. 3)

A forum on the Hills water problems, with 250 people attending, reached no final solutions, but there was agreement that while livestock and wildlife both played a role in the problem, there were other factors equally responsible for depleting the water supply, including forest use and increasing population in and adjacent to the Black Hills (RCJ 19 October 1954, p. 1).

In the late 1950s cooperation between ranchers and the Forest Service was suggested as a solution to the range management problems marking the rehabilitation of ranchers as part of the forest community. A model program began in 1956 with sixteen permittees organizing the Beaver Creek Cattle Association to bring back a high park grazing area and maintain it. The management plan called for fencing the unit into smaller units and using them in rotation to allow some units to lie fallow while others were being actively grazed. They also used aerial spray of herbicide for weed control. The association grazed 1,752 head of cattle on 26,425 acres for 6,425 animal months. (An animal month is a way of gauging the amount of forage one animal needs for one month. Twelve animal months will be represented by both one animal grazing for twelve months and three animals grazing for four months.) Through spraying with the herbicide 2,4D and rotation of the active grazing area, the number of desirable plants on a test plot increased from 9 percent in 1953 to 44 percent in 1958. Forage production increased twenty-four pounds per acre during the same period under the same conditions. The five-year rotation plan called for resting a pasture a full year after weed eradication and then rotating its use during the year for the other four years. The association also hired a herd manager. The program was still considered successful in 1960 (RCJ 16 July 1960, p. 3; 28 July 1960, p. 9; and 7 June 1962, p. 1).

The lesson on the benefits of cooperation and involvement of permittees in management was lost on the Forest Service. In 1962 the Forest Service once again suddenly, and unilaterally, changed its method of issuing grazing permits. These contracts had been issued to grazing districts composed of member ranchers and the district's officers had distributed the permits. Dealing through the districts had reinforced the mutual responsibility of all permittees to maintain the range. When the 1962 contracts were released, they were different in all districts and were to be signed by permittees, not district officers. They were also five-year contracts, not ten-year contracts. The aura of cooperation between grazing districts and the forest service over management plans had disappeared. The Forest Service's absolute authority for management plans was clearly stated in the grazing contract. Ranchers hired lawyers to assert their contractual rights. When lawyers became involved, the Forest Service stopped talking to ranchers and appeals became the method of communication (RCJ 26 April 1962, p. 19; and 9 December 62, p.3). An appeal of one grazing district's lease resulted in the Chief Forester declaring that the Forest Service was only to assist in developing management plans, rather than have the primary responsibility for them (RCJ 3 May 1963, p. 1). The Chief Forester also said that it was the district's responsibility to determine range capacity (ibid.).

Clearly, during this time there was a viable model for preventing the deterioration of range land through cooperation. That this model was not implemented shows that the forest community was not serving in a management role, and the Forest Service did not want that to change.

The ranchers' and farmers' experiences were particularly important in comparing this period from 1920 to the mid-1960s to the earlier common property period. From 1920 to the mid-1960s they were no longer part of a forest community in which the Forest Service and the users of the forest acted as owners and managers. Conflicts developed between users when the sufficiency of the forest browse for both wild and domesticated animals was threatened. When groups worked together, such as when ranchers in a district worked with the Forest Service to improve the grazing land, it looked like a community might form again. However, the management style of the Forest Service could not incorporate users as decision makers. The mutual respect between users of a multiple-use resource was no longer present. Placing blame for browse problems took more time than solving them did. The State Game Departments insisted on having input on decisions affecting wild animals and fish because responsibility had been given to it. However, the connection between wild animal browse, so necessary for sportsmen, and grazing land for ranchers was not automatically seen. It was hard for state and federal officials to acknowledge that browse was a mutually important subject, for which they shared jurisdiction, and this did not even consider the past practice of including ranchers and farmers as full members of the forest community. By the mid-1960s the land was suffering, and related water problems were present. Cooperation among users and managers was not the chosen solution. Formal appeals boards became part of the social structure and a means of communication that would have been unnecessary in a common property resource management scheme.

The Role of the Mining Sector

The period from 1920 to mid-1960s brought major changes in the way mining was treated in the Black Hills National Forest. Mining had reigned supreme as the one resource definition that was beyond the control of even the Forest Service because of the Mining Act of 1872. That act allowed free access to the public domain for the purposes of any mining. Miners did not have to consider other uses of the Forest because they had precedence. They had not really even participated in the common property resource management scheme described earlier. In this period mining changed its own role within the group of users of the forest resources, and forced re-definition of the meaning of "multiple-use," and giving South Dakota a reason to reclaim the right to benefit from national forest resources. The miners' behavior forced the Forest Service to set specific regulations curbing their open-access behavior, and increasing their management presence in the Forest giving and the appearance of more government control over the forest. Mining also caused significant environmental problems through its continued open pollution of water resources.

After 1912 when the school lands were segregated from the National Forest and consolidated into Custer State Park in the southern part of (then) Harney, (now Black Hills) National Forest. The only official interest South Dakota had in the Black Hills National Forest was to enforce the game, fish, and wildlife laws. However, the Great Depression was the catalyst for the State desiring more direct benefit from the Black Hills. As mentioned earlier, most of the population of South Dakota resides in "East River", the area east of the Missouri River. Most of the mineral wealth of the state is in the Black Hills, known as West River. Mining spared the Black Hills counties much of the economic suffering that accompanied the Great Depression in the rest of South Dakota. Only some lignite, bentonite, and sand and gravel were mined commercially outside the Black Hills counties during this period (Lincoln, 1937).

Throughout the depression years the Black Hills were a bright spot on the otherwise dark map of economic conditions in the United States because of its mineral wealth. Most of the wealth was generated by the Homestake Gold Mine. Not surprisingly, the South Dakota state legislature wanted to have the rest of the state benefit from the mining wealth. Until passage of the first ore tax in 1935, South Dakota had not benefited directly from any mining activities in the Black Hills. Certainly there had been an indirect benefit through economic development of the area, but there was no tax of any kind on mineral production. Legislation for an ore tax was aimed at Homestake. The first mention of a severance tax on minerals occurred in 1933. A 10 percent tax was introduced by the Farmer's Union in East River as a way to finance the state government during the depression. The mines threatened to close if the tax was passed (RCJ 19 January 1935, p.1; 30 January 1935, p. 1; 5 February 1935, p.1), and when the governor signed a 4 percent ore tax, residents of West River (the Black Hills and eastern Wyoming) circulated a secession petition (RCJ 26 February 1935, p.1). Despite the threats, the mines stayed open and the Black Hills did not become a separate state. Only Homestake had sufficient production to trigger the tax provision so there was no support for its repeal until it was considered a deterrent to mining development in the late 1950s (RCJ 3 March 1959, p. 13). The imposition of the ore tax was more important for its symbolism than the amount of money it raised, because it included South Dakota in the group entitled to benefit from the Black Hills National Forest.

Miners in this period approached prospecting for minerals other than gold with the same kind of tunnel vision that the gold miners exhibited in the 1870s. They considered the forest only as a potential mine. The federal government had always been a strong advocate for mining in the Black Hills. When the Great Depression spawned a resurgence in prospecting that was unrivaled since the early 1890s (RCJ 7 April 1932, p. 1), one of the questions raised was whether gold claims in game sanctuaries (only established in 1920) would be valid. Both the Harding and Coolidge administrations declared such claims valid on federal land (including the Norbeck Wildlife Preserve), firmly establishing that commercial development took precedence over wildlife refuge within the National Forest (RCJ 25 October 1930, p. 1). Pegmatite mining was also permitted in the wildlife preserve as long as the mining "fully protected wildlife and was at least 660 feet from any highway, so it would be out of view" (RCJ 20 June 1938, p. 8). While South Dakota wanted to share in the mineral proceeds, the state was not willing to make mineral exploration the main use of any or all state land. The governor vetoed a measure that would have permitted mining in Custer State Park (comprised of the school lands severed from the forest in 1912), which is adjacent to the southern Black Hills National Forest, then known as Harney National Forest. The governor said, "Commercial mining has no place in Custer [State Park] and will only result in damage" (RCJ 14 March 1941, p. 1).

Uranium exploration in the 1950s was the catalyst for the change in the federal government's benevolent attitude toward mining claims. The open-access behavior got out of hand when prospectors invaded all areas of the forest with their Geiger counters. It is clear from the enacted regulations that if the miners had considered themselves part of a multiple-use common property resource community, regulation would not have been necessary. The Forest Service had to take some action because, although uranium was important to national defense, the national forest was important to people for activities other than mining, including recreation. Rules and regulations were issued to protect public and private interests within the Forests. The regulations closed public camp and picnic grounds, summer home sites, ranger stations, roadways, and some designated recreation areas to mining activity.

The excesses of the uranium prospectors gave the Forest Service its long-awaited chance to curb use of the forest by miners. In 1954, less than 15 percent of the patented claims on national forests were commercial (RCJ 18 May 1954, p. 1). Mining claims interfered with the administration of the forest by obstructing roads, power lines, and range and timber management. To file a claim only enough minerals had to be found to justify a prudent man to make a further search and do $100 worth of work for five years. When these conditions were met, the miner could patent the claim. Patenting a claim removed the land from the public domain, even if it was heavily timbered.

The national trend in legislation was to discourage privatization of public land, however mining rights remained unchanged (RCJ 18 May 1954, p. 1). Despite protest by the miners, surface rights were legislated by Public Law 167 in 1956. The law gave the government the right to use portions of the mining claim not used in actual mining operation for timber control and access roads. The miner could still use as much of the surface as necessary for mining operation (RCJ 25 March 1957, p. 12). After 1955, the minerals had to be of commercial value for the claim to be valid, and even valid claims were subject to government control of timber-management practices and wildlife conservation (RCJ 20 July 1957, p. 3). Making surface rights on mining claims subject to multiple use was a significant change in resource definition that would eventually help to re-establish a common property resource scheme.

At the same time that miners were losing absolute control over surface rights they started to be held accountable for polluting water resources. Early in this period, in 1929, the Izaak Walton League protested the use of Battle Creek, considered the best trout habitat in the Black Hills, as a waste-disposal vehicle for mines in Keystone. The cyanide was killing fish and vegetation. A bill to protect Black Hills creeks was killed when introduced in the 1928 legislature (RCJ 21 May 1929, p. 1). In 1936 courts affirmed that mining companies had the right to pollute with complete impunity, a right to empty tailings into streams based on the mining custom of the state which dated back to territorial days. Homestake Mining Company even successfully claimed a prescriptive right to pollute based on half of a century of dumping its tailings into Whitewood Creek (RCJ 16 September 1936, p. 1). The Homestake victory came in a case brought by a farmer whose land was severely degraded when Whitewood Creek overflowed onto his land, covering it with mine tailings that hardened to the texture of cement and ruined the land for crops or grazing.

Attitudes about mine pollution changed before the environmental laws changed. One particular example of changing attitudes in 1962 concerned strip-mining of bog iron on National Forest land which caused major acid and iron bonding problems in Rapid Creek. The Game, Fish, and Parks Department of South Dakota thought the strip-mining would cause substantial water pollution, but it did not have adequate data to challenge the practice. The Izaak Walton League supported the strip-mining operation, perhaps to support a local business (RCJ 18 April 1962, p. 2). The miner probably realized that there would be a problem because he restored topsoil to the adjacent private land he strip-mined, but not to National Forest land because there was no requirement to restore topsoil. Preliminary tests showed that water flowing out of the bog-iron site was as acid as grapefruit and was suspected of yielding sulfoxide, a substance toxic to fish. However, the strip-mining went ahead (Rebbeck, RCJ, 4 March 1962). Three years later the scars were still fresh. The top soil was not saved and the acid was leaching into Hop Creek, making it acid, threatening Pactola Reservoir, and increasing sedimentation. That particular mining experience was termed "an experience that taught everyone to stock pile top soil for restoration" (Rebbeck, RCJ 18 October 1964). It was not until 1966 that Game, Fish, and Parks did a study to measure the effects of drainage from bog iron on the growth of fish in Black Hills lakes (RCJ 15 February 1966, p. 1). What the strip-mining did was serve as an example of poor resource management by the miner, acquiesced to by the Forest Service. Private enterprise and mining had won out over water quality and wildlife.

The major changes engendered by mining from 1920 to the mid-1960s were many. It provided South Dakota an entrance into the group vying for forest-management responsibilities. Instead of mining being the primary use of forest land, multiple-uses were required even on mining sites. Environmental awareness of water-supply problems in the Black Hills was also increased. By the end of this period miners, even big mining companies, came to realize that they could no longer treat the forest as their open access mine or use streams as their waste-disposal systems. Miners would have to part of any forest community if one could be re-established.

The Role of the Recreation Sector

Perhaps the most dramatic change in the resource definition of the Black Hills National Forest from the 1920s to the mid-1960s dealt with recreation. Boosterism was a familiar concept within the Black Hills before this time period. In the southern Black Hills, just south of the National Forest, Hot Springs had developed a strong tourist trade based on the warm mineral springs. Aggressive advertising helped. Although the heyday of this attraction ended as the current period began, it certainly provided a model for attracting tourists. The strategy was simple; they advertised not only the health spas, but also the beauty and resources of the Black Hills, the entire National Forest, and Custer State Park, and the healthful ambiance of the area. While this worked well for Hot Springs, it did not benefit the National Forest to any great degree because recreation in the National Forest was geared toward the local preferences of hunting and fishing. It did, however, bring people to the area. The towns of Deadwood, Lead, and Spearfish were also tourist attractions in the northern Black Hills because they had maintained their images as part of the gunslinging, gambling Wild West. In addition to getting tourists to the Black Hills, there had to be something to keep them there for longer than the average two- to three-day stay.

During this period the Black Hills National Forest changed from a passive recreational resource to an active one. Earlier, summer homes, trout fishing, and enjoyment of the scenery constituted recreation in the forest.

Services lagged far behind expectations created by the advertising of the Black Hills as a vacation spot. The secretary of the Black and Yellow Trail (from Chicago to Yellowstone National Park through the Black Hills) warned the Black Hills' tourist industry that they could not simply advertise the existence of the trail, they had to either offer some services or quit advertising (RCJ 12 March 1928, p.5). One concern of tourist industry proponents was how to use the national forest as an attraction. Relying on the beauty of the mountains and scenery was a bad idea. That had worked for the summer-home program, but there were very few summer residents compared with the tourists. By 1934, 154 summer homes had been built on the two forests (RCJ 31 May 1935, p. 1) and most of the permits went to South Dakota residents.

The speaker at a meeting of the Black Hills, Badlands, and Lakes Association told the boosters they had to do more to promote tourism. "They rightly and proudly tell thousands of tourists annually that the Black Hills is the highest point east of the Rocky Mountains. . . . These hills may be the highest mountains east of the Rockies," he (Jack Crampon, director of the Bureau of Business Research at the University of Colorado at Boulder) chided, "but you folks are sitting on the lowest range of mountains in the west" (RCJ 15 October 1963, p. 1). The lakes provided one solution.

There are no natural lakes in the Black Hills (Froiland 1990). Beginning with the Civilian Conservation Corps' work in the early 1930s, and continuing through the Works Progress Administration (WPA) during the 1930s and the conscientious objectors during World War II, public programs constructed of over one hundred lakes and reservoirs. See Figure 12, Sheridan Lake, a man-made lake. The lakes and reservoirs had

Figure 12. Sheridan Lake, built by Public Works Program

multiple roles such as retaining water and fire protection, but they were mainly thought of as recreational assets and a boost to tourism. The creation of these and other recreational and tourist attractions within the forest transformed recreation into a more central role in the resource definition. In 1935 the Forest Supervisor commented on the new lakes as follows:

> The value of all these new bodies of water in the Hills cannot yet be measured. Although they provide pleasant recreational centers for tourists and local residents, their chief value will be in their conservation of moisture. (RCJ 9 April 1935, p. 1)

"Pleasant recreational centers" is an understatement. The lakes provided midwesterners with the novel opportunity to play in lakes in a mountain setting. The three largest manmade lakes, Pactola, Deerfield and Sheridan, completely changed the recreational possibilities in the National Forest, and improved year-round use for both residents and tourists. Of all the lakes, the local population felt most possessive about Sheridan. Although it was built through the Works Progress Administration, it was considered the lake the Izaak Walton League built because the League had re-organized in Rapid City in 1937 for the purpose of obtaining WPA funds to build a lake at Sheridan (RCJ 3 July 1937, p. 1). Because of the lake's proximity to Rapid City, it was used extensively by ice fishermen and skaters in the winter and boaters, swimmers, and fishermen in the summer (RCJ 5 February 1961, p. 23). The three large reservoirs became the recreational core of the National Forest, and water recreation became a major priority (see RCJ 7 May 1966, p. 3).

Most of the campsites within the National Forest were also built in the 1930s as public works projects. The combination of water recreation and campsites increased the recreational usage of the forest. Black Hills residents were the best patrons of the campgrounds from their inception (RCJ 2 December 1937, p. 1). Local residents were so pleased with the lakes that soon after their construction, local people would set up camp in the spring on the best campsites and stay there all summer, usually visiting on weekends, but leaving their camping gear during the week. This practice caused a problem because it tied up campsites, leaving few for tourists. Time limits on staying at a particular site solved this problem.

Throughout the late 1930s and early 1940s, the facilities held up to the demand, but when the public works programs were over, there were no funds for maintenance of the facilities. During the war years, usage was down because of gas rationing, but in the postwar years, the usage of recreational facilities grew steadily. The increased demand created dual problems: there were not enough facilities and the ones that existed had been built by the CCC and WPA and not been maintained (RCJ 7 January 1949, p. 3).

By the 1950s the campsites were in a state of disrepair. Without proper facilities (at least outhouses and fire pits) there was a substantial danger of stream pollution and forest fires. The government sought to address this problem with "Operation Outdoors," a five-year program designed to improve and expand recreation in the National Forests (RCJ 13 October 1957, p. 19). Unfortunately the funds allocated to the Black Hills were only sufficient for maintenance, not expansion. Public outdoor recreation was made a legislative priority in 1962 and 1963 (RCJ 9 December 1962, p. 41), and one of the priorities was to find a way to fund camping facilities. On June 15, 1963 the Forest Service implemented a pilot project to charge $1 per day at selected destination campgrounds. Charges were made only at "prime campgrounds" that furnished flush toilets, electrical outlets, a parking spur, fireplace or grate, and a table. The pilot project was to determine whether charging was feasible. There was no fee for daily recreation (RCJ 14 March 1963, p. 2). The $1 daily fee did not decrease usage at all (RCJ 14 February 1964, p. 3), but it also did not raise enough money to properly maintain the facilities.

Coupled with the deficit in infrastructure maintenance was an increased demand both from the local population, which after 1942 included military personnel stationed at Ellsworth Air Force Base in Rapid City, and a concerted effort to use the national forest as an attraction for tourists. The role of the national forest in tourism development was problematic. Money generated from tourists was part of the benefit stream flowing from the National Forest as a multiple-use resource. There was some tension between private and public interests because, while the Forest Service needed funds to maintain the Forest, the private sector also wanted to reap the benefits of tourism. It was clear that the tourist industry would only tolerate the Forest Service providing what the concessionaires could not provide through their special-use permits. Concessionaires were particularly concerned about competition because of the short tourist season which lasted only seventy to ninety days. (RCJ 14 February 1964, p. 3). However, the burden of providing the tourist infrastructure (roads, lakes, picnic areas, and scenery) fell primarily on the Forest Service and other parts of the public sector, with the private sector reaping the monetary benefits. Outdoor recreation had become a profitable, private, economic activity, contributing $30 million to the state of South Dakota in 1960 (RCJ 5 February 1961, p. 18).

Tourism was an industry that needed an interregional transportation infrastructure to bring the tourists to the Black Hills and an intraregional one to facilitate their enjoyment of the Hills once they arrived. With the demise of passenger rail service, highways were extremely important.

The federal government did fairly well in providing the interregional highways, considering that the Black Hills were one of the few reasons to route highways through western South Dakota and eastern Wyoming. Maintaining and improving roads was more of priority than maintaining camping facilities, although the two were connected. In July 1936 Gutzom Borglum, the sculptor of Mount Rushmore criticized the state's "oxen cart highway system" (RCJ 31 July 1936, p. 1). The Black Hills highways were still in deplorable condition in 1950 and some offices of the American Automobile Association were calling the roads to the Black Hills impassable and telling motorists to take another route instead to Yellowstone (RCJ 19 September 1950 p. 4).

Intraregional highways faced the added problem of needing to be primarily scenic. Pigtails (circular highways shaped like pigtails) were built into the roads in the National Forests to maximize the visitor's opportunity to enjoy the scenery. One dispute arose when a highway through the Black Hills was proposed as a divided, limited-access highway. The Black Hills and Badlands Association did not want it to be divided because that would limit opportunities for tourists to stop, and perhaps stay in the Black Hills once they saw how beautiful they were (RCJ 29 April 1958, p. 1; 5 May 1958, p. 3; and 10 May 1958, p. 1). The scenic highways were very difficult to maintain and in 1961 the Black Hills roads got the poorest ratings in South Dakota (RCJ 12 July 1961, p. 2). The road problem was not solved during this time period.

There were additional problems with other proposed recreation projects. Some of the recreational attractions seemingly conflicted with other established uses of the forest. Hiking trails were criticized severely by private landowners within the Forest as being a "plaything of professional recreationists." They opposed the hiking legislation turning the abandoned narrow-gauge railroad beds into trails, saying that they were not opposed to outdoor recreation, but were opposed to $60 million and a half-million acres set aside for a few hikers at the expense of the food and fiber the rest of us will need in the future (RCJ 10 June 1966, p. 13).

Other conflicts arose over whether to develop recreational areas within the forest or preserve wilderness. One such area was Dark Canyon near Rapid City. Even earlier Dark Canyon was proposed as an area to set aside because it had been special to the Sioux Nation and there were cave drawings there. However, the Forest Service had not set it aside. When the old Crouch Railroad Line was abandoned, the rail bed was suggested as an access route to this unique wilderness area. The Forest Service was asked to make a reconnaissance report because small areas of wilderness were authorized under the U.S. Forest Service Regulations at the time (RCJ 16 May 1949, p. 4). The Forest Service wanted to carefully study what category to put Dark Canyon in and to learn what use the local residents preferred. The Izaak Walton League and several other groups wanted development (RCJ 16 June 1949, p. 4). The reconnaissance report must have taken a long time, because it was not until 1966 that the Forest Service decided to develop Dark Canyon as a primitive area and to keep a wild area open to city residents since it is close to Rapid City (RCJ 19 September 1966, p. 18; 2 October 1966, p. 17). It was not classified as wilderness.

There was a proposal for recreational development of Harney Peak, the highest peak in the Black Hills at 7,242 feet that did much to inspire residents to maintain the status quo in the forest. In 1966 preliminary plans were submitted to the Forest Service for a highway up the southeast side, a tramway up the southwest side, a visitor center at the top, a highway through Grizzly Creek, and improved trail and camping facilities on the perimeter. The Forest Service asked the South Dakota Game, Fish, and Parks Department for its opinion, and its officials said it would reduce the wild mountain goats from a 300 to 400 head herd to 50 to 75 head and drastically reduce the elk. It was estimated that it would increase tourist traffic on the peak from 14,000 people per year to 500,000 per year (RCJ 8 September 1966, p. 1). After public exposure of the plan, the Forest Service decided to keep only the lookout built by the Civilian Conservation Corps on the peak, locate the road to protect the mountain goat habitat, and make the road a scenic drive, rather than a highway. The Forest Service also insisted that Harney Peak eventually needed to be developed to keep people in the Black Hills longer (RCJ 17 December 1966, p. 3).

In the effort to find more things for tourists to do, Indians began to be treated as a tourist attraction. The first suggestion of using Indians was a news story in 1940 about the tourist value of the Indians being neglected (RCJ 17 August 1940, p. 1). Later, a Sioux Sun Dance (sacred to the Sioux) was advertised as a rare opportunity for tourists (RCJ 1 August 1951, p. 1). As a result tourist inquiries about Indians were substantially increased in 1957 (RCJ 16 January 1957, p. 1).

A critical article about Black Hills tourism noted the liabilities of no public transportation, poor facilities, second-rate attractions, and a shortage of lakes and streams for this area which was considered a stopover on the way to Yellowstone. The expert's recommendation was to bill the Black Hills as the "First stop in Indian Country . . . and *regardless of how you feel about them, Indians still have a romantic attraction to easterners and city dwellers* (emphasis added). Promote this angle because it is truly a family attraction, particularly for the kids" (RCJ 19 October 1955, p. 1). In 1962 a tourism expert again suggested making more use of the Indians as a tourist attraction, having more Indians in full dress, and more pow wows (RCJ 8 January 1962, p. 3). The attempt to use Indians for Black Hills tourist publicity was ironic, given the dispute over ownership of the Hills.

The dramatic changes in recreational opportunities during this period raised conflicts about increased human use of the National Forest and added to the groups wanting to make money from use of the National Forest. During the 1920s to the mid-1960s, the Forest belonged to the government when it came to ownership responsibility, but it also belonged to anyone savvy enough to create a way to make money from the forest resources. One issue that had not yet been clarified was whether tourists were part of the benefit stream flowing from the forest or part of the forest community because they had an expectation about Forest use. Clearly, under the earlier common property management scheme, they would not be considered within the ownership community. Lakes and roads were the improvements made during this time period, but maintaining the improvements proved to be beyond the Forest Service resources without some community assistance.

The Addition of Monuments Marking Contested Space

Monuments commemorate events and people of great cultural significance to those who construct them and to those who view them (Harvey 1979; Rowntree and Conkey 1980). Some monuments are significant only to one culture while others have a broader appeal. Some mark the end of conflict and others simply stand as markers of ongoing conflict. Monuments always exist in the past, present, and future contexts.

When and why they were built are part of their original context. Who visits them and what meaning they evoke in their present and historic contexts are often closely tied.

Monuments seldom mean the same thing to all people. In this section, the reader is asked to consider two monuments carved into mountains in the Black Hills, Mount Rushmore and Crazy Horse. These monuments figure prominently in the debate over ownership and sacred space which started as early as 1874 and continues even today.

During this period cultural resources were intentionally added to the Black Hills as monuments to the two cultures that still claimed the Hills, the Sioux Indian Nation and the United States. Although the Sioux Indian claim has not been prominent in earlier discussions of the Black Hills National Forest, it has always hovered in the background. The Sioux Nation never gave up its claim to the Black Hills as their sacred place. All people in the Black Hills seemed to be well aware of that, both in the present and in past accounts of the Hills.

Mount Rushmore was built first. (See Figure 13a.) The timing of the carving, the amount of federal money that went into the project, and the effort to create an aura of sacred space by calling it the "Shrine of Democracy," all can be seen as both a symbol of government ownership and a counterweight to the Sioux contention that the Black Hills

Figure 13a. Mount Rushmore, 1992

were *their* sacred space alone. Mount Rushmore was conceived and promoted as a tourist attraction, but also symbolically extended the group claiming ownership rights beyond the residents of the Black Hills to all patriotic Americans. Crazy Horse (see Fig. 13b), on the other hand, was conceived of and promoted for its symbolic statement—that the Sioux claimed ownership of the Black Hills—and it became a tourist attraction as a way to finance its construction. Together these monuments identified the Black Hills as contested space. They clearly stated that the United States and the Sioux Nation both claimed the Black Hills as their own.

Today the Hills's dominant culture is white, Euro-American, and the largest minority is composed of members of the Lakota Sioux Indian Nation. Although the relationship between the Sioux Nation, and the U.S. government, and the dominant culture in the Black Hills are much better by comparison than they were in the late 1800s, there is still tension over the ownership of the Hills. Reasonable people on both sides continue to differ on who "owns" them (Lazarus 1991). Some still claim that the U.S. Government's taking of the Hills was legal, despite the Supreme Court decision that it was not legal, but the Sioux were only left with monetary damages, not the Hills (Ibid.). Some claim that the Sioux never rightfully held the Black Hills because they had improperly taken them from other Indians (Parker 1984). Some members of the

Figure 13b. Crazy Horse Memorial, 1992

Sioux Nation feel that they should accept the damage award and close the case, while others believe that land is not a commodity, and this particular land is sacred and therefore would never be sold under any circumstances.

This section focuses only on the context in which two monuments were created and how their cultural meaning has developed. The thesis is that the monuments are symbols of contested meaning and contested ownership. The Euro-American culture used the construction of Mount Rushmore to stamp the Hills with a symbol of U.S. ownership and control and to create the aura that the Black Hills were sacred in the white culture. The Crazy Horse monument was the Indian's response to Mount Rushmore.

In 1920 Congress passed the Sioux Jurisdictional Act authorizing the Court of Claims to hear equitable and legal claims against the United States. In 1922 the Sioux hired an attorney, and in 1923 he filed twenty-four compensation claims, the largest of which was for their sacred territory. Newspaper articles from that period demonstrated that the Sioux legal action was a threat to the whites (Lazarus 1991). With the beginning of the construction of Crazy Horse, the Sioux openly expressed their claim to a place in the forest community.

Carving a monument to the great leaders of the United States was proposed from outside the Black Hills region by South Dakota's state historian Doane Robinson and U.S. Senator Peter Norbeck as a way to attract people to the Black Hills. Even though Mount Rushmore was couched in blatantly commercial terms from the beginning, there may have been other motives because the project started at approximately the time the Sioux Indians hired a lawyer to file their compensation claims for the taking of the Black Hills. From the beginning, Mount Rushmore was both a state and federal project.

The idea of carving a mountain was not immediately popular with local residents (RCJ 28 December 1924, p. 11), but after intense lobbying, the Black Hills Pioneers came out in favor of the project (RCJ 3 February 1925, p. 1). The local commercial clubs prorated sculptor Gutzom Borglum's expenses and Keystone financed a road to Mount Rushmore (RCJ 14 September 1925, p. 1). The commercial clubs assigned Hills towns quotas of money to raise for the effort (RCJ 20 April 1927, p. 1). In 1926 President Coolidge was invited to set up the next summer's White House in the Black Hills. Part of the impetus for bringing the Coolidge White House there was to get federal support for Mount Rushmore. In August 1927 President Coolidge gave a speech at the monument site and laid the groundwork for later claims that is was a sacred space for American patriots:

> The people of the future will see history and art combined to portray the spirit of patriotism. . . . This memorial will be another national shrine to which future generations will repair to declare their continuing allegiance to independence, to self government, to freedom and to economic justice. (Fite 1952)

In March 1928 a bill was introduced to create a Mount Rushmore National Memorial Commission and ask for $250,000 in federal funding (RCJ 30 March 1928, p. 1) and in February 1929 the Senate approved the Mount Rushmore project (RCJ 22 February 1929, p. 1). Even during the Great Depression, Mount Rushmore received federal funds from the government (RCJ 22 September 1932, p. 1). This use of federal funds is particularly interesting in light of the rejection of the Forest Service's request for $150,000 for labor to reseed the forest, a project necessary because of some devastating fires.

Lest there be any mistake about the political meaning of choosing Presidents Washington, Jefferson, Lincoln, and Theodore Roosevelt, Borglum made it perfectly clear in 1936 that "Mount Rushmore is a monument to the men who had founded, defended and expanded the United States" (RCJ 9 December 1936, p. 1). Eleanor Roosevelt had asked him to put Susan B. Anthony on Mt. Rushmore. He said he would "brush that request aside as he would an annoying fly on a wet day" (RCJ 17 January 1950, p. 7).

When Rapid City residents made an argument for becoming the second capitol of the United States in 1950 they listed ten reasons and number 10 was "In event of extreme emergency following an invasion, what more appropriate spot could be found for the final defense of democratic government than in the shade of Mount Rushmore, the National Shrine of Democracy" (RCJ 1 March 1950, p. 4).

The Crazy Horse monument was the Sioux Nation's counter to Mount Rushmore. In 1939 Chief Henry Standing Bear, on behalf of Sioux Nation chiefs, asked Korczak Ziolkowski, an award-winning sculptor, to carve the monument of Crazy Horse out of one of the Black Hills mountains to show the white men that the Indians, also, have heroes (Lazarus 1991). This work was undertaken privately, without government financial support and with some government suspicion.

The Crazy Horse monument did not become a matter of public record until after World War II. A *Rapid City Journal* headline on March 26,

1947 announced: "Monument to Indians Proposed for Hills, Larger than Mt. Rushmore" and the dateline was Washington, D.C. U.S. Representative Case clearly saw Crazy Horse as a rival to Rushmore. In April 1947, he told his constituents:

> ... while I think the Sioux are entitled to have a great memorial I would not seek federal funds to finance it; (I think) that Rushmore has yet to be finished; that if the federal treasury has more money for Indian projects, too many Indians need homes to spend federal funds for this purpose.

The matter was left with all understanding that the forest service and Indian services would consider the conditions they might suggest before giving their informal blessing to the project. (RCJ 15 April 1947, p. 4)

Work started without federal funding, but it was difficult and slow. Ziolkowski bought a ranch near Custer for $4,000 and moved there with his family. He chose Thunderhead Mountain and filed a mining claim. The Department of the Interior told him that the department would arrange for setting aside 360 acres of the National Forest as a national monument and they would still hold title, but Ziolkowski would have the exclusive right to mine. Ziolkowski said, "The government might get around to financing a monument a hundred years from then when noble red men were near extinction, but the project can't wait 100 years" (Fite 1952). He had looked for a suitable place at Pine Ridge (the Ogalala Sioux Reservation), but could not find one. The Black Hills were also more appropriate because they were Crazy Horse country. The Sioux Indians used the Black Hills to hunt, die, and seek refuge from whites and it was appropriate that the monument be there because Crazy Horse was not a reservation Indian. (RCJ 7 November 1947, p. 1).

There was controversy about the monument in both the white and Indian communities. At first the white community was very hostile, because the Indians refused to give up their claim and because they said the monument to Crazy Horse was going to be so big that Mount Rushmore would fit in Crazy Horse's eye. The white community came to believe that there were some benefits, however, from tourism. A petition signed by a large number of Custer businessmen asked the South Dakota congressional delegation to support a loan of $250,000 to the Crazy Horse Memorial Commission. This was a switch from May 1957 when the banner across Custer's Main Street directing tourists to Crazy Horse was removed (RCJ 27 June 1957, p. 1). There was a decided lack of local promotion and cooperation and no federal support. News Reporting continued to concentrate on hearings on the Sioux claims (RCJ

21 June 1953, p. 2) with occasional articles opposing any payment to the Indians tribes for treaty lands (RCJ 27 February 1956, p. 10). Another matter that came to light in 1955 was the 1942 bombing of the Pine Ridge Reservation. In July 31, 1942 the War Department ordered the Indians to leave their homes at Potato Creek because it had become a target range. This started the modern Indian exodus from the area (RCJ 2 July 1950, reported to a congressional committee in 1955, RCJ 13 September 1955).

Perhaps because of Crazy Horse, people became more protective of Mount Rushmore, and the idea that Mount Rushmore was a sacred place crept into the public consciousness. A Joe Palooka comic strip featured Mount Rushmore and the people of the Black Hills were upset because it was a mockery of the Shrine of Democracy (RCJ 18 December 1947, p. 1). The trustees of Mount Rushmore complained about the cartoon saying it was a mocking of a sacred American memorial. A former United States Attorney said "I consider Mount Rushmore a sacred place. I consider it profane to place the Shrine of Democracy in the funny papers" (RCJ 20 December 1947, p. 1). Later, Senator Case criticized the desecration of the shrine of democracy in *North by Northwest,* an Alfred Hitchcock film, because Cary Grant climbed on (a mock-up of) the sculpture (RCJ 22 August 1959, p. 1). Commercial use of the Shrine of Democracy later became acceptable. There was no outcry when an advertisement for Washington's Birthday sales included a picture of Mount Rushmore with George cut out and a caption stating that he went to the birthday sale in Rapid City (RCJ 18 February 1966, p. 1). By 1992 Mount Rushmore was featured in a television weed remover commercial with someone spraying weeds growing out of Washington's nose with herbicide. In 1995 a toothpaste company illustrated the effectiveness of their product by brushing the teeth of all of the presidents on the monument. Mount Rushmore did its job drawing visitors and most were from out of state. In 1957, a sample of 3,000 cars showed the average visit was forty-seven minutes. Thirty-two percent had seen the shrine before, only 36 percent visited the museum, and 67 percent visited concessions (RCJ 10 February 1957, p. 1).

The ultimate plan for Crazy Horse is for a cultural center dedicated to North American Indians, a university and medical school, and the large monument (Crazy Horse promotional pamphlet, 1992). Both Mount Rushmore and Crazy Horse are now outside the bounds of the Black Hills National Forest, although they were originally within the bounds.

Changes in this Non-Common Property Period

In this period from 1920 to the mid-1960s the Black Hills National Forest reverted back to being a government-owned and -managed resource. The forest was managed more tightly than in the last period. The Forest Service preferred to deal with fewer people on timber contracts, support fewer, but more established businesses, and take away the power of grazing districts.

Many new definitions were added, mostly at public expense. The lakes and reservoirs brought the addition of water-based recreation. The CCC and the WPA did priceless work on thinning the forest and building an infrastructure. Highway construction made all other uses easier. The addition of the monuments made the controversy about the history of the ownership of the Black Hills public.

The users of the forest had lost their sense of responsibility for caring for the forest. The Forest Service had taken control of decisions and was left with all maintenance responsibilities once public programs ended, which were beyond its capabilities. The forest had not reverted to an open-access resource, but it had become a government resource once again, having lost its common property character. This period closely resembled the early years of the Black Hills National Forest, before it came under the influence of Gifford Pinchot. This period also served as a catalyst to change the management style for the Forest as is illustrated by the next chapter.

Chapter 5

Reconstructing a Forest Community

From the late 1960s until the early 1980s was a time of dramatic change in environmental awareness in the United States. After Rachel Carson's *Silent Spring* was published in 1962, people started thinking about the state of the physical environment and how the earth was being used by humans. There was popular pressure to conduct discussions about humans and the physical environment that would fall within Anthony Giddens' category of discursive consciousness. The routineness of past environmental behaviors was questioned when people were confronted with the results of such behavior. The first Earth Day was held in 1969, marking a national commitment to consider the earth when making decisions.

The original study behind this book treated the late 1960s until 1985 as the last period of study. In the Black Hills National Forest there had been a period of environmental problems that could no longer be ignored by the late 1960s and were being addressed by the mid-1980s through active user involvement in management and maintenance. There was a semblence of a resurgent forest community by 1985. The forest community in this period had to be much different from the one in 1905–19 because the population of the Black Hills was significantly different in size and economic complexity. Forest users were less likely to be individual multiple-use users than they were in the earlier period. The National Forest was no longer the centerpiece of the economy for the region, although it still held a prominent place, especially with the growth of the tourist industry.

National environmental groups also had a great impact not only on local attidudes, but also on congressional attitudes, as shown by the several pieces of legislation passed in this time period. These included the National Environmental Protection Act (NEPA) in 1969, which required an environmental impact assessment on all projects altering the physical environment. The stream of legislation was punctuated by court involvement. The most significant case concerned clearcutting in the Monongahela National Forest in West Virginia. This case was filed in 1971, and the Fourth Circuit Court of Appeals in 1973 decided against clearcutting as a primary management practice. Clearcutting results in even-aged stands of forest and the court decided that such a management practice was beyond the discretion of the Forest Service. The case precipitated the adoption of the National Forest Management Act (NFMA) by Congress in 1976, which required all National Forests to file management plans, not final until they had been commented on by the public. The plans included not just timber, grazing, watershed management, and recreation, but also required an inventory of and consideration of cultural resources in the area. The Native American Freedom of Religion Act of 1978, required consideration of sacred sites, even if they had not been used for years because of exclusion by other uses of the National Forests, which precluded Native American religious ceremonies. Appeals processes accompanied all of the new legislation. Issues that were ignored in the past had to be considered under the new regulations for the National Forests. Cultural resources had to be inventoried, which in the Black Hills meant that prior use of the forest by the Sioux Indians could no longer be ignored just because the Sioux did not live within the "human resource unit" surrounding the Black Hills National Forest.

In this period there were hints that a forest community was being reborn as more people living in the area took interest in how the forest was being used. There were also struggles between federal, state, and local groups over control of the forest. One of the issues was again, was the Forest "everyone's," meaning an open-access resource or was it going to be a common property resource with an ownership group that did not include everyone, or did it belong to the government? Before the late 1960s the Izaak Walton League was the only organized group dedicated to policing the physical environment in the Black Hills. By the end of this period the Sierra Club had formed a local chapter bringing a national presence of environmentalism. Outside of these organizations, people in the Black Hills communities took an active interest in how the forest was to be used because it was so much a part of their landscape, both physical and cultural.

The question of whether there would be another common property period was not fully answered by 1985, and now there is additional material that shows how the process of resource definition has progressed.

The State of the Forest in the Late 1960s

The condition of the Black Hills National Forest by the mid- to late 1960s reflected unsustainable use patterns and a deterioration of the health of the forest as a whole. During the non-common property period between World War I and the mid-1960s, each major use of the forest was defined and managed separately, and exploited as fully as possible with a particular goal in mind. The interrelationships among the uses were neglected. The price of that neglect was loss of the Forest's multiple-use definition, heated competition between users, and substantial environmental degradation as a result of the many uses of the Forest, as shown through the condition of the watershed. Environmental problems were actually the catalyst for renewal of the multiple-use concept and reconstruction of the forest community.

The need to revamp the operational definition of multiple use became obvious when people started to unravel the causes of environmental degradation in the Black Hills and take a hard look at how the forest was being used. Several environmental problems were related to the narrowed resource definitions, adopted during the previous period. Most notably, water quality and quantity had deteriorated due to abuse by each of the prescribed groups of users. The water problems were symptomatic of the larger problem that the forest was no longer a multiple-use resource but a place for several resource-consuming uses. Users and managers had lost sight of the interdependence of uses. Consequently, the health of the forest as a whole was neglected. This chapter examines the water crisis as the catalyst for change, the process of redefining "multiple use" and the process of reconstructing a forest community around a multiple-use common property resource.

The Water Crisis

> Water is an essential element in the use and management of other renewable resources in the Black Hills. Demand for water far exceeds supply, and will continue to do so. Careful consideration will be necessary in the allocation and use of water in order to achieve optimum harmonious and coordinated management with other resources. This is the key to successful multiple use. *(Black Hills Area Resource Report,* 1967:225)

Although essential to all uses, very little was known about the water situation in the Black Hills. No hydrology studies were done until the

1970s. Since 1957 the South Dakota Game, Fish, and Parks Department had been trying to sound the alarm that the watershed was being neglected, but until the problems became overwhelming, there was no support for a change.

The precipitating event that triggered action on the water crisis was the loss of trout streams and the threat this loss presented to the sport-fishing industry and the image of the Black Hills. Trout served the same role as canaries had in mines; canaries were the first to die in mines when the air was unhealthy, likewise if the trout died, the stream must be unable to support life. The 1,200 miles of trout streams in the Black Hills had been reduced in 1965 to a mere 200 miles, and during 1965 another 15 miles were lost because of diminution of water quantity (Rebbeck, RCJ 10 November 1965).

In 1965 the South Dakota Game, Fish, and Parks Department conducted a water inventory in the Black Hills that described the sorry state of streams and noted some of the causes. Quantity problems were attributed to the closed forest canopy rather than grazing, as had been the case in the the 1930s and 1940s. Water-quality problems had multiple causes: mine waste which contributed silt and chemicals; agricultural activities, which disturbed riparian vegetation, causing erosion of the banks, as well as agricultural pollution; siltation of the streams and organic pollution; road construction, which contributed to siltation and pollution, especially when forest roads were built along stream beds; and summer homes, recreation facilities, and occasionally, entire communities that dumped raw sewage into the streams (RCJ 23 May 1965, p. 39; Stewart and Thilenius 1965).

Although the focus of concern was the threat to sport fishing, the ramifications of the water problem were much greater. The lakes and reservoirs endangered by siltation and eutrophication would be lost to all uses, irrigation as well as other forms of recreation. A 1967 comprehensive study of the natural resources commented on how there had never been any significant hydrology studies of the area (U.S. Department of Agriculture, et al., 1967).

Although the streams were damaged, they were not irreparably damaged. With considerable effort it was possible to rejuvenate them. The leading success story was 2.8 miles of the Stockade Beaver Creek headwaters. The Forest Service considered their rehabilitation task because they were the sole owner, but its sole ownership raises serious questions about how the stream could have become degraded under its watchful eyes.

In at least one forest district, the Elk Mountain District, watershed became the central concern and the other uses, grazing, timber cutting, and road building, were geared to protect the watershed. This model watershed area was the same area where deteriorated range conditions had prompted stockmen and the Forest Service to enter into a partnership of intensive management ten years earlier. As part of that management scheme a rotation grazing system was set up and the stream was fenced to protect streamside vegetation. Another major benefit to the stream was relocation of the road, closing and seeding over the old road, and having culverts empty into grassed areas. Before the rehabilitation, trout could not live in the stream and afterward, it became one of the more heavily used sport-fishing areas in the summer and fall (RCJ 5 November 1967, p. 17). It is obvious from these examples that not only did stream rehabilitation have to employ multiple-use principles, but that the problem had multiple causes.

Employing multiple-use principles for watershed management was not always an easy process because of the pressure single-interest use groups could wield. The Black Hills Water Management Study was completed only after an entire volume was removed because the public objected so strenuously to its recommendations. The opposed provisions were that grazing and farming be restricted along streams in the higher Black Hills; portions of trout streams be fenced and easements for fishermen be obtained with money from the sale of trout stamps (like fishing permits); cultivated soils be classed as an industrial source of pollutants; and a West River Waste Treatment Authority be created. The people were disturbed by the anti-agriculture position that went against their image of themselves as farmers on the frontier (RCJ 28 January 1976, p. 2). The lack of total public support for the cleanup process was a major hindrance to any comprehensive water plan.

Redefining Multiple Use

As the understanding of environmental problems broadened, criticism mounted toward the narrowed resource definitions being applied in the Black Hills National Forest by both the Forest Service and the S. D. Game, Fish, and Parks Department. Criticism was directed at the practice of targetting only one aspect of a resource use category for management. The two examples discussed here are: defining fishing exclusively as trout fishing, and defining timber exclusively as ponderosa pine. The former was a decision by the Game, Fish, and Parks Department, which had jurisdiction over fish and wildlife management in the national forest, and the latter was a decision of the Forest Service.

Trout are not native to the Black Hills. While they can survive under the conditions found there, they presented the state with several limitations because they were the center of attention for the sport-fishing industry. As discussed earlier, trout need relatively clean water and even with clean water, they must be stocked or "planted" annually in the lakes and streams because they will not reproduce in the Black Hills. Other fish, native to the Black Hills, but not considered good sport fish, ate the trout almost as soon as they were released. The standard management practice was to eradicate all of the fish in a lake by poisoning them with rotonone in the fall, making the lake safe for trout the next spring. This practice had been carried on at least since 1950.

In 1973 state fish biologists wanted to treat Sheridan Lake with rotonone, but they were presented with a petition signed by four hundred people asking that Sheridan be allowed to remain a mixed-fish lake. The petitioners claimed that the Game, Fish, and Parks Department was biased against warm-water fish and that making a lake a "trout-only" lake took away from its character as a "family lake" (RCJ 27 March 1973 p. 1). Biodiversity had not yet entered the vernacular. A straw vote of 95 to 3 against poisoning the lake at a Game, Fish, and Parks Department-sponsored meeting resulted in cancellation of the plan. The state agreed to continue to stock trout, but noted that most would be lost to predation (RCJ 29 March 1973, p. 1). Some lakes, where there was no public protest, continued to be poisoned with rotonone. Iron Creek Lake, built by the Works Progress Administration in 1936, was treated at the request of fishermen when test nettings in 1980 showed that 92 percent of the fish in the lake were suckers, natural predators of trout (RCJ 7 August 1983, p. 1).

Hardwoods in the Black Hills faced the same fate as native fish. Figure 14 shows a stand of quaking aspen, one of the prominent hardwood species. They were routinely eradicated in favor of more desirable trees, in this case, the commercially marketable ponderosa pine. A virtual monoculture of ponderosa pine was being intentionally created, much to the satisfaction of the timber industry. There were no complaints about the narrowing definition of timber pondersosa pine until 1966 when the Forest Service embarked on an aggressive campaign to remove aspen, starting what was known as the "Aspen War" in the Black Hills. The intention was to annually bulldoze or chemically spray one thousand acres of oak and aspen to make way for a new age class of commercial pine. Hardwood eradication was within the federal guidelines for National Forests. Since 1956, 5,385 acres of hardwood had been eradicated under similar plans (RCJ 25 June 1966, p. 1).

Figure 14. Aspen Stand

There were two lines of argument against removing aspen: first, it was destructive of the forest as a whole by substantially depleting the wildlife habitat; and second, it was not even the most cost-effective way of increasing ponderosa pine growth. By removing hardwoods to make way for a pine monoculture, the Forest Service and the lumber industry had incorporated their narrow-use patterns into a redefinition of the forest. They ignored all functions of trees in a forest except that of commercial harvest. The protesters of this redefinition paid most attention to the wildlife habitat role of aspen, perhaps because state game officials and several outdoors groups were well organized to lead the fight. Aspen provided deer and elk browse and a habitat for the ruffed grouse and wild turkeys. In addition to the loss of habitat, bulldozing the hardwoods stripped vegetation, ruined trout streams, and contributed to siltation of streams and reservoirs. It cost $55 per acre to eradicate hardwoods and only half that to thin an acre of pine, with similar results (Rebbeck, RCJ 10 June 1966).

Aspen removal was halted to study its effect on wildlife habitats after the protest. The Forest Service promised to cooperate with the state Game, Fish, and Parks Department more closely on wildlife needs. They said that if studies proved wildlife needed aspen, they would consider it in future management decisions (RCJ 24 June 1966, p. 1). In fact, studies showing the importance of aspen for deer habitat had already been conducted in 1946 and in 1966 (RCJ 26 June 1966, p. 1).

The central term of the truce in the Aspen War gave the state Game, Fish, and Parks Department the right to review Forest Service work plans through official lines of communication (RCJ 25 June 1966, p. 1). Once a cooperative system was established, timber and browse were easily accomodated through adherence to multiple-use principles.

In 1967 the Department of Agriculture and the Department of the Interior conducted the "Black Hills Area Resources Study" and identified ways that natural resources could be used for the economic development of the area. The resource uses identified in the study were the same uses that had been identified all along: recreation, mining, agriculture, timber, and watershed management. The key to the new multiple-use definition was in the connections between uses. Illustrations of the redefined multiple-use definition are provided by looking at the new roles of timber, mining, and roads in the forest.

The Role of Timber in the Redefinition

The core position of timber in the Black Hills had long been recognized:

> Forestry is the mainspring in management of the interwoven biological resources of the Black Hills. Generally, what is good for timber production is also good for livestock, wildlife, water production, recreation and what is good for each is good for the economy. (Rebbeck 16 January 1966).

When timber production became redefined as logging pondersosa pine, it lost its connectedness with the other parts of the resource definition. The focal point of restoring the interconnectedness of timber was thinning the pine. Figure 15 shows a thinned stand of pine. When pine stands were not thinned, the closed canopy diminished the water budget, crowded out other species, and diminished browse, and the doghair stands were a fire danger. Stockmen referred to the pine as "that weed." The benefits of thinning had been well demonstrated in the Civilian Conservation Corps era, but since then, thinning had presented two problems: who would do the thinning, and what benefit would they get? Whenever public service job funds were available, requests were put in for thinning in the Black Hills (RCJ 24 February 1983, p. 1), but funds were not readily available in the same way they were during the New Deal.

The multiple benefits of thinning brought pressure for thinning from many directions. Thinning would raise the water budget, encourage the growth of browse for wildlife in the winter and livestock in the summer, and act as a check on fire danger. The antithinning contingent was the

Figure 15. Thinned Stand of Ponderosa Pine, 1992

timber industry, the group designated to do the thinning as part of their timber contracts. The sawmill industry (see Fig. 16) complained bitterly about having to harvest the roundwood along with the saw logs because it added to their costs and did not have a market. Timber operators continually lobbied for looser requirements for disposal of small trees, complaining that the Forest Service was emphasizing aesthetics and recreation over their livelihood (RCJ 28 June 1982, p. 1). The Forest Service maintained that they had built in a higher contract price to compensate for handling roundwood as well as timber and that it was unacceptable to simply cut and leave roundwood on the contract sites.

The Forest Service, through Black Hills National Forest management and through the Rocky Mountain Experiment Station, went to great lengths to develop a market for roundwood that would make thinning operations cost-effective, if not profitable (Boldt and VanDeusan 1976). The leading new uses were particle board (Markstrom, Lehmann, and McNatt 1976) and plywood (Donnelly and Worth 1981; RCJ 6 May 1969, p. 1). Pulpwood continued to be shipped to midwestern pulpmills with favorable rail rates, and during the national energy crisis of the early 1980s when the price of oil skyrocketed, the residents of the Black Hills made significant use of roundwood for firewood (RCJ 1 November 1981, p. 1). Sawmill waste products (particle board and plywood, for example) also became the basis for new industries that

Figure 16. Lumber Company, Hill City, Custer County, SD, 1992

were suggested by the U. S. Department of Agriculture (RCJ 20 November 1978, p. 1; 10 February 1981, p. 2).

While the volume of roundwood the timber industry had to handle would always be an issue, the interconnectedness of timber with the other uses of the forest was firmly reestablished during this time period.

The Role of Mining in the Redefinition

The biggest change in mining as it met with the multiple-use redefinition of the Black Hills National Forest was that it came to be seen as a "two-sided coin." The economic benefits were appreciated, but environmental damage was the more immediate local concern (RCJ 20 March 1977, p. 25). Even economic benefits were closely scrutinized. Mining was not very good at producing tax revenue, as shown by the ore tax results in the 1930s. Furthermore, most of the workers were transients who did not even own property (RCJ 14 April 1975, p. 2). On the other side of the coin, several reports by the mining companies had shown that upwards of 75 percent of purchases for mining needs were met within South Dakota. Before local communities would allow mining, they wanted to make sure that they would not be stuck with unusable land when the mining was over. The way to ensure that in the national forest was to force mining into the multiple-use fold.

South Dakota became the advocate of the people for protecting even the Black Hills National Forest from the excesses of the unchecked, open-access mentality of the mining industry. South Dakota enacted a surface mining law in 1973 with the following legislative intent:

> The development and extraction of these minerals by means of surface mining is necessary for the economic development of the state and the nation, and proper safeguards must be provided by the state that, upon the depletion of the mineral resources, the affected land is usable and productive to the extent possible for agricultural or recreational pursuits or future resource development: that water resources are not endangered; and that aesthetics and a tax base are maintained, all for the health, safety and general welfare of the people of the state.

Although the law need not have applied to National Forest land, the Forest Service said it would enforce the stricter regulations (RCJ 14 March 1975, p. 2). Willingness of the Forest Service to enforce the state rules suggests that it recognized the problems caused by mining in the National Forest that had not been previously addressed.

Whenever a major mining project surfaced, even in the planning stages, local residents were certain to raise questions about its effect on water quality, reclamation plans, and the quality of life in the area. A proposed taconite mine near Nemo, in the northern Black Hills, is a good example of the quality of scrutiny exercised by the local populace. The mining permit filed by the company called for removal of a four hundred-foot mountain, seven million tons of rock and creating an open pit below the valley floor. The *Rapid City Journal* ran a nine-part series on the proposed mining project that highlighted the concerns of the parties. The people of Lawrence County (center of Black Hills mining and home of the Homestake Mining Company) opposed the permit because they thought large-scale mining would disrupt other values, recreation and tourism, fish and wildlife, forestry, and agriculture. The mining plan was dormant for several years while it was tied up in court on an appeal by South Dakota. But when Pittsburg Pacific Co. reactivated their interest, so did the people by forming "Concerned Citizens for Nemo" (RCJ 4 June 1979, pp. 1–2). After 1979 there was no further mention of the Nemo project.

Another example of forcing the mining industry to recognize mining as only one of the multiple uses of the Black Hills dealt with the uranium mining industry. Even after the Forest Service obtained the right to manage surface rights on mining claims, the uranium industry presented many problems regarding multiple use. Although uranium was considered very important becausee of its role in nuclear power, there were concerns about radiation and contamination of the water supply.

Primarily the southern part of the National Forest had uranium potential. The Elk Mountain District of the BHNF was in the "uranium district," where exploration had suggested large deposits. In the late 1970s there was still a good market for uranium and several multinational corporations were interested in the Black Hills. Union Carbide's attempt to mine Craven Canyon precipitated the formation of a local forest community intent on preserving the Black Hills as a multiple-use resource. A group known as the "Black Hills Alliance," formed to oppose uranium mining in the Hills (RCJ 16 June 1979, p. 3), appealed permits granted to Union Carbide and tried to get a veto for voters on uranium permits. By 1982 the bottom had fallen out of the uranium market, so plans were abandoned, but there was a lasting sense of empowerment for the people who lived in the Black Hills region.

Holding mining accountable as part of a multiple-use forest community was not really a task the Forest Service felt it should take on. In 1983 the National Wildlife Federation challenged the Forest Service's contention that they could not regulate mining in the national forest because the 1872 Mining Act gave that authority to the Bureau of Land Mangement. The federation wanted the Forest Service to do more to protect water quality and wildlife habitat. The forest community reconstituted during this time took on the role that the Forest Service was reluctant to assume. Through activities aimed at controlling mining, the forest community was actually strengthened and better prepared to assume responsibility in a management scheme. Even gold prospectors were held accountable for stream damage caused by placer mines. Reclamation plans had to include restoring trout streams to the satisfaction of the trout (RCJ, 8 October 1982, p. v-3).

Having the Forest Service monitor damage from mining and its willingness to adopt state game regulations are evidence that the Forest Service was again becoming a member of the forest community, not the controller of the forest. South Dakota was also pushing hard to become a member of the forest community.

The Role of Roads in the Redefinition

Another major catalyst for renewing the commitment to a multiple-use definition was forest roads. Road building had been a priority in forest management since the beginning of the national forest. Roads were essential for timber harvest, mining, and fire control, and greatly enhanced the accessibility of grazing ranges and recreational sites.

Multiple use of roads was both an advantage and a disadvantage for the definition of the forest as a resource. Although roads were constructed with one purpose in mind, usually timber harvest, they were used in other ways as soon as they opened. Roads opened previously undeveloped areas to recreational uses that were often not environmentally sound. Many people, particularly those in the northern Hills and the Limestone District, wanted to keep some of the National Forest undeveloped for wilderness-type recreation. In the late 1970s the public told the Forest Service that they wanted fewer, not more roads, through two federally mandated public-inventory processes called Roadless Area Review and Evaluation (RARE I and Rare II). The Forest Service said that one of the problems they faced in transportation planning was that the public changed its mind from wanting roads to not wanting roads (Riley 15 February 1979).

Obliteration of roads after timber sales was one of the major points of compromise. A three-year plan, reported in 1979, called for closing nine hundred miles of road either by returning the road bed to its natural vegetation or by means of locked gates that allowed access for only fire and maintenance vehicles and protected wintering animals (RCJ 3 October 1979, p. 38). The problem was preventing roads from being used by cars and four-wheel-drive vehicles even after they were officially closed. (Riley, 12 November 1978). Winter closing of roads was also a rule, but the Forest Service assigned one hundred miles of trails to be maintained by both the South Dakota Department of Wildlife, Parks and Forestry and Westriver Snowmobile Council (for use as snowmobile trails) (RCJ 24 November 1978, p.V-3).

There never was agreement on the roads issue, but what made it important in the redefinition process was its multi-use aspect. Future roads had to be considered in terms of their primary purpose and their contributions, intended and unintended, to multiple use.

The New Forest Community

There were two critical elements in the reconstruction of the multiple-use common property system: 1) acknowledgement and appreciation for the interdependence of uses, and 2) establishment of a community of users with control over the use of the resource and management responsibilities. A new forest community developed in this period, emerging on its own through the pressure of the local populace and sometimes in the face of Forest Service opposition. The federal laws, National Environmental Protection Act, and the National Forest Management Act both had provisions requiring public involvement in forest management. Single focus groups did not drop out of the picture, but they were held accountable by other members of the community for their impact on other uses and users as well as their impact on the forest as a whole.

The reconstituted forest community was much more complex than the original one established from 1905–19. This new community included state agencies regulating mining and water quality, economic-development planning groups, federal agencies other than the Forest Service, local interest groups, user groups, and the general public. The Forest Service had to share management decisions with the community, and that was a difficult transition. This transition probably was not fully made in this time period. What emerged was the beginning of an institution for managing a common property resource much like the ones described as successful common property institutions by Ostrom in chapter 1.

Perhaps the biggest change in the forest community was that by 1992, the Forest Service had lost control over its composition. Throughout the previous non-common property period, the Forest Service had defined the forest community as the users it worked with. It had appointed the Forest Advisory Group, and it controlled what "public" would be consulted about forest management. This practice came under severe criticism in the late 1960s and early 1970s. One form of implicit criticism was the establishing of user groups such as the Black Hills Forest Resources Association. The Association was formed in 1967 by sawmill operators, post-and-pole plant operators, and pulpwood operators for the purpose of encouraging management practices that would assure continuing benefits to all from private and public forests. The group wanted an inventory of timber resources and had a long-range goal to create "public understanding that rising pressure on all forest land to meet increasing needs for timber, water, recreation, wildlife habitat, minerals, forage and other values can be accommodated best by sharing these uses of the land under sound forest management" (RCJ 29 March 1967, p. 16). Another example was the Black Hills Alliance, organized in opposition to uranium mining in the Black Hills, including mining within the national forest.

In 1972 the Forest Service, realizing that public support was crucial, embarked on an "inform and involve" public relations program. The idea was to institute area planning, to inform the public of the management problems, and to involve them in future planning. The public meetings were geared toward management of particular areas and were scheduled at various locations throughout the Forest (RCJ 11 January 1972, p. 2). The write-up on the first round of public meetings was positive. The Pactola District meeting was sponsored by the Izaak Walton League and management problems discussed included coping with large numbers of people and campground maintenance. Management rationale and future infrastructure needs were explained to the public (RCJ 22 January 1972, p. 25). Although newspaper articles were mostly positive, letters to the editor suggested that the public was not quite in favor of the process. One woman from Deadwood wrote:

> I don't pretend to be very smart, but I still can see a little ways beyond my nose. It's obvious that the Forest Service is trying to passify [sic] the people by holding these public meetings 'to inform the public of their management programs and to get the people's point of view', when all they are doing is feeding the public a bunch of promises that are never kept. (RCJ 1 March 1972, p. 5)

Some changes in management plans were made after public comment. The Spearfish District plan was revised after public meetings where people asked that wilderness be maintained. Some of the roads that the Forest Service had planned to improve were closed (RCJ 19 April 1972, p. 11). However, other criticism continued to come out in letters to the editor. Closing campgrounds because of lack of maintenance funds was questioned when large sums were being spent on logging roads. The closings were called an infringement on people's rights by big government bureaus (From Letter to the Editor by Leroy Seyhers, RCJ 24 May 1974, p. 5).

The openness of the public comment proceedings could be questioned based on the following question to the *Rapid City Journal's* "Action Line":

> Why is the Forest Service, an agency administering public land, holding question and answer meetings in various districts of the Black Hills to discuss policies and doing this by invitation and excluding the general public? E.K., Hill City

Action Line answer:

> Because they don't want to deal with groups of from 150 to 200 people and have the meeting develop into a "adversary meeting" like the one in Custer last month, according to Del Harding the forest's information officer.

Mathers wanted to collect information on how the public felt about the forest service, but he wanted it from a "true cross section of public sentiment." (RCJ 13 December 1978. p. 6). Rangers invited ten to twelve

people to meetings based on their feeling that the people were representative of the community. Others were welcome to send in their written comments anytime.

The public had several avenues of comment besides Forest Service
sponsored meetings. One particularly effective avenue was through
state government agencies which came to be advocates for environmental responsibility with the National Forest and were responsive to
complaints about Forest Service management from the local population. There was considerable comanagement between the state and federal government in the National Forest because of the state's responsibility for wildlife, noted above. Acceptance of the state presence in the
forest was inevitable, and during this period the state joined the forest
community as regulators and managers. The state agencies were not always in opposition to the Forest Service. For example, the Game, Fish,
and Parks Department strongly endorsed the 1976 ten-year timber plan
that raised the allowable cut to 190 million board feet a year, thereby
enhancing both water and forage availability. They particularly liked
the selective road closure and leaving relatively large tracts for wildlife
(RCJ 18 May 1976, p. 2).

The National Environmental Policy Act of 1969 gave the public an
"in" on the ground floor of policy with the national forests through environmental impact statement requirement. There were eight points of
public involvement scheduled, beginning with solicitation of what the
public thought were the issues and concerns. The final environmental
impact statement that accompanied the first forest plan under the National Forest Management Act of 1976 (NFMA)(Forest Service 1981)
contains a list of all of the people who commented on the plan and
many of the comments themselves. The level of participation evident
from that document and related news articles suggests that the public
felt free to participate in the planning process. The plan was not hard
to understand, as this review of the environmental impact statement
states:

> Bulky, detailed, exhaustive as the environmental impact statement may
> be, it isn't really hard to understand. More wood, its says. Fewer moun-
> tain pine beetles. More aspen. More grazing. And fewer roads, in the
> long run. Nicer scenery. More and cleaner water. In short, a healthier for-
> est. (Rebbeck, 10 April 1976)

The alternatives were briefly summarized and, it was noted how a person could get a copy of the plan.

Indians were still excluded from the forest community. Some Sioux tried to force their way into the forest community through occupation of the Yellow Thunder Camp on the National Forest. The Forest Service's attempt to remove them from the site was the subject of much publicity and court action from 1973 through the the present. At one point in 1973, the American Indian Movement camped out at Mount Rushmore, as much for symbolic and publicity reasons as any other. They were required to leave that site and established the camp as a religious site. They wanted to build a permanent camp, basing their right to do so under the Native American Freedom of Religion Act of 1978. The Forest Service was adamantly opposed to setting aside part of the Forest exclusively for the Indian group. Although the Indians won in the lower court, they eventually lost their appeal, but more important than the outcome was the Sioux demand that they be part of the forest community. This demand could not be denied with the National Forest Management Act requirement that there be a cultural resources inventory which was carried out by Cassells, Miller, and Miller (1984). This report catalogues not only sites of Indian use, but the continued claim by the Sioux that the Black Hills as a whole were sacred, not that there were a few sacred sites. The report also contained information about the Yellow Thunder Trial as well as differing opinions of scholars about when and how the Sioux claimed the Hills and whether their claims could be proven. Such debate in 1984 did not help racial relations, especially since it appeared that the Forest Service did not intend to honor Sioux claims. The Sioux claims of ownership were found true by the United States Court of Claims 1979 and the United States Supreme Court in 1980. However, the claims have never been settled, because under U.S. law, the Sioux Nation is only entitled to monetary award and the Sioux want the Black Hills. Senator Bill Bradley (D-N.J.) has introduced bills in Congress to return only the publically owned portions of the Black Hills to the Sioux Nation (Lazarus 1991). The Sioux claim of present entitlement to the Black Hills is still a topic for hot debate in the area as well as a cultural matter to be considered in Forest Management Plans. The problem is that the Euro-American planners want specific sites to designate as sacred sites, and the Sioux Nation views the Black Hills as the "Center of Everything That Is" (Charging Eagle and Zeilinger 1987). The Sioux book, *Black Hills, Sacred Hills* (ibid.) contains few words and many pictures, while most Euro-American books about the Sioux Claims contain many words and few pictures (Lazarus 1991). The cultural gulf is enormous and the Black Hills National Forest sits in the middle of it.

Almost every Forest Service action in this period helped to further define the forest community by identifying who felt entitled to oppose its plan in the name of preserving the multiple-use character of the forest. A proposed tramway up Harney Peak was one example discussed earlier. A Colorado corporation had proposed a recreational/cultural development of Sylvan Lake and Harney Peak. (RCJ 19 March 1970, p. 25; and Forest Service memoranda). They had been studying the site since 1965. Development at Harney Peak would include a visitor's center at the Peak, the highest elevation in the Black Hills at 7,242 feet, hiking trails and a Plains Indian cultural center, a state historical museum, and an amphitheater at Sylvan Lake. It was designed to retain the semiwilderness character of the region and blend in with the physical environment as much as possible. There were several objections to the project, including complaints that a Plains Indian Center did not belong in the Black Hills (Newby undated), and that it would bring too many people to the area. Because of this proposal, which seemed to be favored by the Forest Service at first, a Sierra Club was formed and there was a strong campaign to keep outsiders, specifically Colorado residents from developing the Black Hills National Forest. The project was abandoned in the planning stage.

One of the challenges to development of a complete forest community in this period was that the general public obstructed the formation of a true common property forest community by their open-access behavior and refusal to participate meaningfully in a sustainable management plan. Senator Tom Daschle (D-S.D.) supported open-access claims to recreation without consideration of their ramifications for the forest as a whole. The overt problem was the issue of fees for recreational use of the forest. In 1973 an executive order, by then President Richard Nixon, eliminated fees on most national forest campgrounds, saying that fees could only be charged if flush toilets, showers, sewage disposal, visitor protection, access roads, designated camping spaces, refuse containers, and drinking water were provided. On the Black Hills National Forest that meant that only Sheridan Lake could charge fees (RCJ 9 August 1973, p. 1). An editorial in the *Rapid City Journal* on August 15, 1975 said that Congress did no one any favors by wiping out the fee schedule because someone had to pay for facilities and the proper thing to do would have been to lower standards for what fees could be charged, not to encourage more facilities. "Campers, like stockmen, should pay for use," the editorial stated (RCJ 15 August

1975, p. 12). The editor's view was not widely shared only a few years later when the fee plan was implemented for Sheridan Lake.

Sheridan Lake was the most used lake in the Black Hills because of its size and proximity to Rapid City. As a manmade lake it had silt and eutrophication problems, and preserving it took considerable work. A fee plan for Sheridan Lake was proposed in 1984 for using boat launches and beaches on the north side of the lake. Local people opposed the plan, but the Forest Service decided to implement it anyway because it would save the government money (Singsaas 1987). The fees, paid to a concessionaire, were not high: $1.25 per day for a boat launch, $25 for a season pass good at both Sheridan Lake and Pactola Reservoir; beach use was $2 per day per carload; picnic use cost $3 per day; the camping fee stayed at $6.50 per day and included use of the beach. The Forest Service's share of the concessions was 17.5 percent, about $16,000 for the season. A fee program had already been in effect at Pactola for several years without opposition (Willis, 25 April 1984).

There was a fundamental misunderstanding about how National Forests are funded. The president of Black Hills Fish Bandits opposed the fees because people had to pay both at the gate and through taxes. But, does payment of taxes sustain the Black Hills National Forest? All other user groups paid modest fees for the privilege not the right of reaping benefit from the National Forests. People who went to the beach after the fees were implemented complained about paying them, but still went. Use was down a little, but the weather was also cold (RCJ 1 July 1984, p. 1). A meeting of three hundred people challenged the Forest Service on the fees on July 4, 1984. Senator Daschle called the meeting and told the crowd that it was not fair to charge the fees to those who have already paid through taxes. It was wrong to balance the budget on the backs of those who use Sheridan Lake. "We've paid for it once" was the popular refrain. The Izaak Walton League was angry about private concessions because they had bought the land for the lake and given it to the Forest Service. Public opinion, however, was not unanimous, some supporters of the fees said the area had been improved by the concession. Daschle vowed to fight the fees all the way. One opinion reported in the *Rapid City Journal* was that the Forest Service didn't own the land, the public did (Willis, 5 July 1984), but there was no suggestion that the public should in any way perform management tasks. The fee appeal was successful and the fees were dropped after October 1, 1984. However, for the remainder of the 1984 summer season the public harassed the ticket takers at the Lake in a very abusive way (RCJ 2 August 1984, pp.1–2).

Even though the Forest Service backed down, they expected Congress to give them more authority to set fees in 1985 (RCJ 31 December 1984, p. 2). The Reagan administration proposed across-the-board recreational user fees in 1985 (RCJ 14 February 1985, p. 2). Daschle again vowed to fight the user-fee proposals and took much credit for ending the pilot program on user fees earlier. Despite their unwillingness to pay, the public wanted more services. They wanted year-round access to campgrounds and picnic areas (Taylor, 9 June 1985). Traffic control was a major problem in 1985 because the road usage had risen again and there was nowhere to park (RCJ 24 June 1985, p. 3). New parking lots paid for with the Forest Service's budget, were the solution (RCJ 9 June 1985, p. 3). With strong public opposition, the concession program had no chance for success (Singsaas 1987). The public claimed the right to use the forest recreationally, but felt no commensurate duty to maintain the recreation areas.

Thoughts about the Period from the Late 1960s to 1985

In the final analysis this period ended without the reestablishment of a full common property resource (CPR) scheme. The forest community as reconstituted had many of the attributes of a common property group. Multiple use was clearly defined; and the user group was clearly defined. However, the missing link was the inability to count on all those who availed themselves of the benefit stream from the forest to also have management responsibilities and participate in sustainable use.

As long as the public felt entitled to open access based on their taxpayer status, there could not really be a forest community. Recreation was expensive to support with roads, parking lots, and siltation problems in the manmade reservoirs. It did not contribute any revenue and really freeloaded on the back of the other uses. This open-access mentality remained the biggest impediment to the formation of a forest community. In other ways the public seemed to act as if they were members of a forest community: they evaluated uses according to whether they would enhance or detract from the multiple-use concept. They kept single-use interests accountable for their place in a multiple-use community, but they had a major blind spot when it came to recreation. They used the public access provisions of the National Environmental Policy Act and the National Forest Management Act very effectively to support their version of a multiple-use resource, but they just as effectively used their political influence to create an open-access recreational niche for themselves to the detriment of the establishment of a true common property community. Whether or not the Black Hills National Forest can be used in a sustainable manner as a multiple-use resource in the future depends to a great degree on whether a full CPR community can be reestablished.

Life under the Forest Plan—1985–1993

After adoption of the Forest Plan the big question was, would it work? That question had to be answered for each forest separately because the local communities potentially had such a large influence on the contents and enforcement of the Plans. Implementation of the Forest Plan in the Black Hills National Forest went well in some ways and not so well in other ways.

In October 1989 the Forest Service published its "Five Year Evaluation of the Black Hills National Forest Plan, 1984–1989." The evaluation raised two major problems: there was not enough money to carry out all planned activities, and wilderness became a major bone of contention between the Forest Service and both most multiple users and wilderness advocates. It should be noted that the five year evaluation was an internal Forest Service document. Each issue raised in the original Forest Plan was considered under the following format:

1. How the issue is addressed in the Plan.
2. How the Plan has been implemented.
3. How the issue has changed or how demand had changed.
4. Conclusions and need for Plan Revision. (Forest Service, 1989:1)

Most of the actions that would implement the Plan were either in the early implementation stage or had been postponed because of lack of funds. One of the more interesting parts of the report concerned the condition of the soil cover in the Forest, measured by monitoring transects in timber sale areas, clear-cuts, skid trails, and slopes steeper than 40 percent (ibid at 4). They found that "transects taken in timber sales logged with rubber-tired or crawler tractors had about 25 percent bare ground and 75 percent ground cover" (Ibid). To deal with this problem, skid trails needed to be seeded and water-barred to reduce soil erosion. In wildfire areas it was found that natural revegetation would not be enough to establish adequate ground cover even after four years because annual weeds were the only vegetation that returned after being part of a monitored wildfire burn after three years. Suggested future changes included active reseeding of burns where the slope was greater than 50 percent.

Water-quality and -quantity goals were complicated by a drought from 1985–88, but the Forest Service was still trying to get money for a hydrology study. The conclusion of the Department's evaluation was that more resources needed to be focused on water quantity.

Fish and wildlife issues were addressed through active cooperation with South Dakota's Game, Fish, and Wildlife Department, and local sports groups. This cooperative planning for wildlife habitat before timber sales went out to bid. Emphasis on wildlife had become a greater priority nationwide since the Plan was adopted, so more attention needed to be directed at wildlife habitat. Wildlife studies had not been completed within the first five years of the plan because adequate money had not been allocated and there was no relief in sight (id. at 13).

Mining was an issue of intense public interest, because of its visibility to the public and its historical impact on the quality of water. The Forest Service tried to discourage requests to withdraw more land from new mineral entries public concern about the negative aspects of mining on ground cover continued to be in the forefront of discussion about public lands (id at 15).

Developed recreational sites were a continual overload on Forest Service resources because of greater demand for more luxury in camping services. The Forest Service thought the private sector should handle this. In 1988 the Forest Service had to respond to a nationwide initiative on recreation. With present resources it was unable to satisfy public demand and planned to turn to the private sector for help in meeting the demand. One of the problems for the Forest Service was that demand was strongly influenced through marketing by such organizations as the South Dakota Campground Coalition, over which it had no control.

An even greater problem than campground conditions was posed by off-highway vehicles using, and sometimes creating a twenty-three hundred mile primitive road system in the forest. Increased hiking trails were provided by the Rails to Trails program which converted abandoned railroad beds into hiking trails. It is curious that the major problem concerning public use of the Forest for recreation was "visual management," meaning to not keep evidence of clear-cutting away from public view, for example, because it was necessary for water-quantity enhancement, but would be misunderstood by the public. The report noted that residents of the Black Hills did not like to see changes in the way the Forest looked (id. at 24). It also noted that wilderness use had been over reported, a foreshadowing for the fight yet to come over wilderness with the Sierra Club.

Grazing was an area that needed more money for monitoring. Only 78 percent of the grazing allotment was being satisfactorily managed in 1988 (id. at 28). Cattle had to be tagged with large colored tags to identify the ones that were registered in the Forest.

Timber harvest fell below what had been projected in the Forest Plan, and while much of the error was attributed to errors in calculating the timberland base, this was a major public issue. The chief concern was that many small lumber businesses and sawmills had planned their future on the timber projections contained in the Plan, and found that they could not survive under the real conditions of less timber availability.

Development around the Forest boundaries was another area that needed to be addressed because the area was becoming suburbanized, and the Forest Service was concerned about how many additional demands would be put on it. More attention needed to be paid to adjacent ownership. What used to be adjacent farms and ranches in the 1905–19 common property period was adjacent subdivisions in the late 1980s. The problem was that once agricultural lands became private homesteads in the early 1900s, they were forever removed from the National Forest and were unconditionally private. With the demise of small farms, much former agricultural land was turned into vacation home lots or year-round retirement homes.

Norbeck Wildlife Preserve was created out of the Black Hills National Forest by an act of Congress on June 5, 1920. It is adjacent to Custer State Park and its management in complementary to Custer State Park. The Norbeck Wildlife Preserve includes the Black Elk Wilderness Area, which has been designated officially as wilderness under the Wilderness Act of 1964. In 1927 a master plan was filed for the preserve that included timber harvesting on a 35-year cycle as an integral part of managing wildlife habitat and thinning, and insect control for the scenic value of the preserve. Public campgrounds, summer homesites, and grazing were permitted as long as there was no interference with game animals. In 1932 the Upper Pine Creek Research Natural Area was set aside to preserve an area of virgin timber that could serve as a comparison to cutover land. Most of the area was withdrawn from mineral entry in 1962. A new plan for Norbeck was approved by the Forest Supervisor in 1973, but its implementation was blocked by a lawsuit filed by the Sierra Club (USDA 1979, p. 3). In 1979 a Final Environmental Impact Statement (USDA 1979) was filed that recommended continued management of the Norbeck Wildlife Preserve, including logging parts of it to maintain the wildlife habitat. In the plan's revision process in the early 1990s the issue was whether it should be a wilderness or not.

The wilderness issue is very important because wilderness land is managed by not being managed. When a forest like the Black Hills National Forest is not managed it means that the trees are not thinned, the canopy closes, infestations of insects are not treated, and wildfires are only minimally contained to prevent them from spreading out of the wilderness area.

During the plan's revision the treatment of the Norbeck Wildlife Preserve and the wilderness issue was a point of contention. Public comments on plan revision, some given in a "Hearing Before the Committee on Small Business, One Hundred Third Congress, First Session on Hearing on Public Land Use Impact on Small Business, September 4, 1993," demonstrated how the issue was framed in the eyes of Hills users. The issue was really framed as wilderness versus multiple use, and the multiple-use advocates were able to articulate what multiple use meant and why additional wilderness did not fit the definition.

The Black Hills, Badlands, and Lakes Association, a consortium of 560 small businesses in western South Dakota strongly supported the Forest Plan. The spokesman said that about four million nonresidents visit the Black Hills each year because they are "intimate mountains," not too high, well developed for recreation without being commercial, and they satisfy most of the "city slicker" tourists who visit them. (Senate Hearing 103–380, pp. 53–4.) On the wilderness issue the spokesman said:

> The ornery thing about federal wilderness is that it creates exclusionary zones. Wilderness sets up exclusive preserves for select outdoors men who have the skills, and the stamina and the time to penetrate these tracts, and seek the solitude they crave. . . . Wilderness is off limits to handicapped, elderly, or infirm people. (Ibid.)

The Public Lands Council, composed of 251 people having permits on the Black Hills National Forest, saw logging and grazing as interdependent because of the need to keep an open canopy. They opposed more wilderness because it would be off limits to grazing and felt that it was much better to have more than one use of the forest land at the same time.

Another group that gave testimony was the Black Hills Regional Multiple Use Coalition composed of twenty-nine organizations representing hunters, trappers, snowmobilers, off-road riders, four-wheelers, the forest products industry, livestock producers, mining interests, irrigators, trailriders, conservation districts, and economic-development organizations that have about twenty thousand people as members or employees of members. The existence and diversity of this group is impressive by itself in terms of the level of community organization shown in the time since the first forest plan. It insisted that the definition of the ecosystem should include both a healthy economy and social components as well as the forest ecology. To that end it supported the proposed plan and strongly opposed adding any wilderness. It echoed the concerns of others who testified that it would be economically disastrous to replace timber-mining- and grazing-related jobs with tourist jobs that only last three to four months and were notorious for only paying minimum wage and no benefits (id. at 99–106). It filed a detailed response to each section of the Revised Forest Plan, urging continued public (organizations and individuals) involvement in the planning process, creation of a resource inventory, as much multiple use of the land as possible, and no additional wilderness. The multiple-use group also was concerened that too many frivolous appeals were made of management decisions.

The Black Hills Coalition of Women in Timber also testified about the need to encourage multiple use and maintain a healthy forest products industry. The group spoke against adding wilderness because in the present wilderness preserves there is no forage for the wildlife, so wildlife have abandoned them in favor of managed forest or gardens that provide food. The group also pointed out that the old growth timber the Sierra Club referred to on the Norbeck Wildlife Preserve was mostly about six inches in diameter and was found in dense, stunted stands.

However, not all parties supported the proposed plan revision and opposed wilderness. The Izaak Walton League cautioned that commodity production would not be overemphasized and that there should be some wilderness in the BHNF. The Sierra Club advocated five new wilderness areas and backed up their requests with threats of litigation. They wanted more nonmotorized recreation, less logging and higher minimum rotation ages (growing times) for the timber sales. The spokesman for the group called the BHNF the "most developed, suburbanized, intensively managed" forest in the National Forest system (id. at 65). Others complained that only a few lumber companies were allowed to get Forest Service timber contracts and that the Forest should support more small businesses. Still others complained that the hearing process was not open because there was no open microphone, only invited speakers.

The comments of Senator Daschle were telling. He sent written testimony calling for "a good balance between a variety of uses of our public lands, including logging, mining, grazing, hunting and fishing, and recreation" (id. at 132). It seems that by his phrasing, he is still singling out recreation as different from the other uses. U.S. Representative Tim Johnson, also of South Dakota, called for a fair, common-sense balance between environmental and economic issues (ibid.). Neither official took a wilderness position.

The process of defining the Black Hills National Forest as a multiple-use resource will never be over. In this round of controversy wilderness is the issue, and it seems to have solidified acceptance of a definition of multiple use that does not include much, if any, wilderness. A great deal of doubt was cast that any area in the Black Hills is truly wilderness, especially if one uses the definition of an area unaltered by humans. There are roads all through the Black Hills. The Black Hills were settled before the National Forest was created and any land that was agricultural was excluded from the Forest. Therefore, one is never far from private land or roadways anywhere.

The emerging forest community is quite different from the one that existed from 1905 to 1919. Today's forest community is composed of organizations. The social networks have grown beyond individual connections to encompass larger interest groups. They seem to have a clear idea of "multiple use" as an integrative term, not excluding parts of the Forest from any uses if possible. They view the Sierra Club members as outsiders, even though some long-time Black Hills residents are members. They will not tolerate the preclusion of some of the uses by others, which is what happened when mines did not treat their waste. Accountability is to the group as a whole. The Forest Service is more central than it was in 1905 to 1919, but an increased willingness to litigate decisions is a strong incentive for it to join with a cohesive forest community. It is interesting that South Dakota still offers to take over management of the National Forest any chance it gets, in the tradition of western states wanting the federal government to stay out of their territory (Mercer, 1995). The results of the first Forest Plan suggest that present public interest is strong, and people feel empowered to be involved in the forest community. The multiple-use definition is one that the community likes and seems willing to fight to keep. It is particularly encouraging to hear groups calling for people to be considered part of the ecosystem.

Chapter 6

How Would National Forests Gain by Using a Common Property Framework?

Federal ownership of land probably will never be popular, especially in the western United States. The Sagebrush Rebellion and continuous opposition to fees for federal land use match the states' desire to take over National Forest land. States want both the land and the revenue as well as the absence of federal authorities. To get past the state/federal barrier, there must be a partnership including not only government agencies, but also the users of the National Forest. A common property scheme allows for that partnership. Using a common property resource (CPR) framework to conceptualize national forests would focus attention on the statutory multiple use definition. It would offer people access to a benefit stream from the forest and also require them to participate in the management of the Forest. It is a model that allows the Forest Service, state natural resource departments, farmers, sawmill operators, miners, and recreationists to be accountable to the whole forest community. Accepting a forest community does away with the need for posturing between state and federal interests. It implies that groups will work together. The conflict between state's rights and federalism is older than the National Forests, and it is still present.

By now Garrett Hardin himself has given up the inevitability of the "Tragedy of the Commons" by distinguishing between open-access resources and common property resources. National Forests have never been open-access resources; they have always been multiple-use resources open to those who fit within statutory uses. Some of the single-purpose CPRs have become degraded since the studies on them were written in the 1980s. Some of the reasons for that include the non-recognition of the common property resource nature of the resources, such as when states open fishing to people outside the fishing community, creating an open-access resource.

There is no need for such problems to dismantle a common property scheme for a multiple-use resource. This study demonstrates that instead of leading to the degradation of resources, a common property scheme can be an effective way to maintain sustainable use of a multiple-use resource. An effective common property resource management scheme requires that careful attention be paid to the resource definition, the composition of the community entitled to benefit from the resource, and full participation in a management plan.

It is difficult to sustain a multiple-use resource as a common property resource because of the ever-changing definition of resources. It would be impossible to sustain a multiple-use open-access resource because of the lack of formal and informal controls limiting its use and enforcing the resource definition.

From the time of its inception in 1898 to the present, the Black Hills National Forest has been called a multiple-use resource. Although the broad categories of multiple use remained fairly consistent, the overall definition of the forest as a resource was not consistent.

The process of resource definition and its relationship to sustainable use of the forest was examined by using a CPR framework. The questions presented within this framework were: How was the resource defined? What were the boundaries (if any) of the community entitled to exploit the forest within the resource definition? Was there a sustainable management plan?

The Forest Service, usually the center of national forest studies, was viewed not as the owner of the national forest, but as a part (albeit an important part) of the community defining and managing the forest. The study focussed on users and uses of the Black Hills National Forest. Changes in both the multiple-use definition and the forest community provided opportunities to test whether the forest was really a CPR and whether being a common property resource made a difference in the sustainability of the Forest's use.

The overall conclusion is that use was most sustainable when the forest was viewed as a multiple-use common property resource. Specifically, the forest environment was sustainable when it was defined as an integrated multiple-use resource, with intentional consideration of the relationship of each separate use to every other use and to the forest as a whole, and when a forest community, composed of users and the local Forest Service was responsible for development and implementation of a sustainable-use management plan.

National forest policy was only one factor in the resource definition. The first common property resource period occurred about seventy years before the National Forest Management Act of 1976 required multiple-use planning. The implications of the study are important to the management of both other U.S. national forests and protected natural resource areas being used for sustainable development in less-developed countries. Commitment to an integrated multiple-use definition and involvement of the broadly defined user community are the keys to sustainable use of the forest.

Figures 17 through 20 summarize the analysis of the resource definition process and use patterns for the Black Hills National Forest. In the early years of the Black Hills National Forest (Figure 17) mining overwhelmed all other potential uses of the forest. The Forest Service spent much of that period trying to establish ownership over the forest, trying to make all use decisions, and taking responsibility for all management

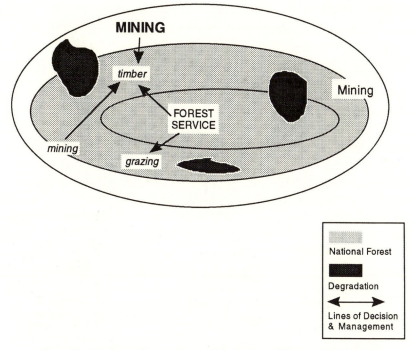

Figure 17. Model of Early Black Hills National Forest (1898–1905)

and maintenance. By statute the forest was a multiple use resource, but mining had a strong influence over timber, and the Forest Service had no control over mining activities. The national forest was clearly established as an entity, but the Forest Service could not control the whole forest on its own.

Figure 18 depicts the Simple Common Property Period between 1905 and 1919. This period began with the transfer of administrative responsibility for the national forests from the Department of Interior to the Department of Agriculture and implementation of the active multiple-use definition advocated by Pinchot and other conservationists of the period. There was a conscious effort during this period to establish a forest community and entrust it with the task of both defining the forest as a multiple-use resource and managing it together with the Forest Service. There was a strong emphasis on hiring local men for forest service jobs which helped integrate the forest community. Migration was a key part of establishing the multiple-use community and lessening the influence of mining, although mining remained very important.

The original common property forest community was primarily composed of multiple users and its uses were complementary. Homesteaders not only had grazing rights, but they also used timber for build-

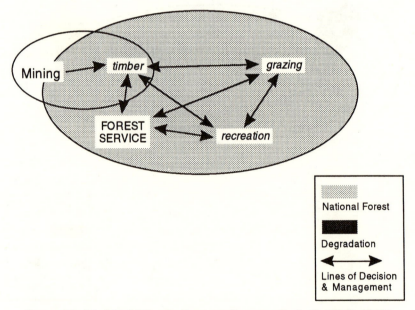

Figure 18. Model of "Simple Common Property Period" (1905–1919)

ing and roundwood for fuel and fence posts. Their multiple use helped thin the forest, clear slash, and protect against fire. Many of them also held timber contracts and sold wood to sawmills. Some also did a little prospecting on the side. Timber operators were local people supplying an exclusively local market. During this period the Forest Service was in partnership with the forest users for the common goal of using the forest in sustainable, multiple ways. The demise of this simple common property community was the central role of outside redefinition of the forest as an economic-development resource, a redefinition that contributed to the breakdown of the forest community.

Beginning about 1920, the forest was divided into separate resource elements (Figure 19). During this long non-common property period the uses were managed and used separately. Timber, through the "working circle" concept, was supposed to be the tool for stabilizing the economies of towns and cities within the forest boundary. Unfortunately it also created a single interest group of timber users which split off from the multiple-use forest community. That group interacted directly with the Forest Service on timber regulation. Grazing districts, particularly after the Taylor Grazing Act in 1934, became the vehicle for managing grazing interests on the forest. Again, a single interest group was created to manage one aspect of the forest with the Forest Service. When the Forest Service gained control of the surface management of mining claims, the mining industry was treated as a segment of the centrally managed forest region. During this period recreational facilities were created, including reservoirs as well as Mount Rushmore and Crazy Horse. Recreation became a dominant use, although not a dominant revenue source. As each use was managed separately, even though it was managed by one unit, the impact on the whole was neglected, and some important aspects of the resource definition of the forest were neglected.

The watershed regions suffered the most during this period, because all interest groups were using them, but no one considered them part of their management responsibility. The Forest Service was in more of a central position than it had been in the 1905–19 common property period. One of the ironic things about this period is that it included the adoption of the Multiple Use and Sustained Yield Act of 1960, and yet the multiple-use definition disintegrated into a "many uses" definition. Exploiting the forest as an economic-development tool encouraged conceptualizing it not as an integrated whole, but as the sum of its exploitable parts.

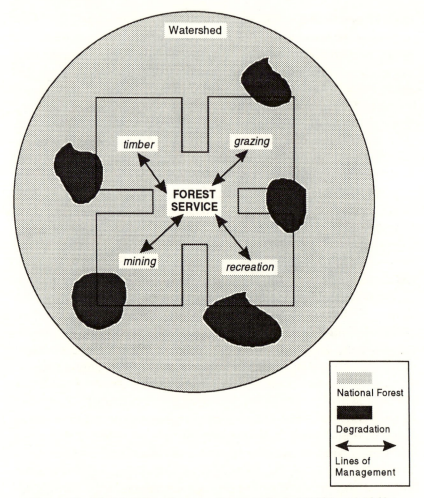

Figure 19. Model of Non-Common Property Period (1920-mid-1960s)

The antidote to the non-common property period was an attempt to re-establish a forest community as outlined in Figure 20. This time, the local populace, instead of the Forest Service, was behind the effort to define the forest community. The forest community established in this second common property period was composed of single-definition users with a fairly clear vision of the multiple-use scheme. They were interested in one benefit stream for their own profit, but realized that their use depended on everyone else's use. The transition back toward a common property scheme was not smooth nor has it been completed.

Uses conflicted with each other, and it was difficult for the Forest Service to cope with an empowered forest community. Both the National Environmental Policy Act of 1969 and the National Forest Management Act of 1976 enhanced the role of the local population in managing the national forests. The role recreational users chose for themselves hampered the establishment of a true common property forest community. Recreational users (primarily users of the reservoirs) treated the forest as an open-access resource that someone else (namely, the Forest Service and other forest users) was expected to maintain. Their refusal to participate in a management plan as full members of a forest community sabotaged the effective re-establishment of a CPR management scheme. Their successful opposition to recreational fees was simply a symptom of their lack of understanding about how the forest could be maintained and sustained. For there to be a common property scheme, the users must also be the managers and maintainers.

The implementation of the first forest plan from 1985 through the present indicates how the resource-definition process occurred under the formal planning process. The nature of the forest as a multiple-use resource became firmer. For example, "multiple use" meant simultaneous uses in the same area of the forest. Disagreement about this definition came from people who wanted more wilderness set aside, and the forest community rose up to challenge the legitimacy of wilderness as a use in a multiple-use forest and the status of wilderness advocates. One of the resentments of the people who considered themselves members of the multiple use community was the ready access "those outsiders" had to the federal court system. The courts were not within the forest community, and yet they had become the ultimate arbiter of the definition of "multiple-use." Given the place of courts in today's society, it is unlikely that an internal conflict-management scheme will ever preclude access to the outside authority by people who feel excluded from the community decision-making process. In the last period studied, people of the Black Hills not only clearly articulated the multiple-use definition, they specifically included the needs of people in the forest community, calling people part of the National Forest ecosystem. The inclusion of people marks an addition to the multiple-use definition, because it encompasses users as well as what is used. The recreational use of national forests still needs to be better defined so that recreational users are either seen as members of the forest community who also have management responsibility, or they are seen as part of

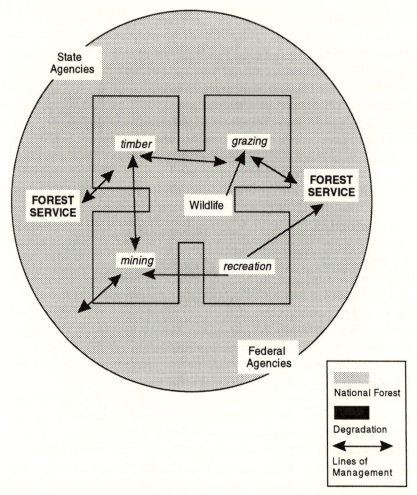

Figure 20. Approaching a Common Property Period (late 1960s-present)

the benefit stream, people without management responsibilities who are simply consumers who pay a price.

The Benefits of the Common Property Framework for All National Forests

The common property framework allows examination of a multiple-use resource definition process which must occur in National Forests. Adoption of the integrated multiple-use definition was even more important than the number of users. National forests, as containers of resources, need to be seen as more than the sum of their elements. The common property framework would be an extremely valuable one to consciously apply to national forest management. Unconsciously it has been applied and worked well in the past. Forest users need to understand the concept and consciously become members of the forest community. It must be clear that public and private "ownership," in the sense of the right to benefit from use of a resource, are not mutually exclusive. Successful common property management uses both public and private enforcement principles. Defining the resource and defining the community entitled to benefit from it, and responsible for maintaining it, are the most important steps in forming a sustainable use plan for a complex multiple-use resource. The common property framework provides a model for designing sustainable use.

Bibliography

Acheson, James M. *Lobster Gangs of Maine*. Dover, N.H.: University of New England, 1988.

Alleger, C. N. *Civilian Conservation Corps, South Dakota District History*. Rapid City, S.D.: Johnston & Bordewyk, Inc., 1935.

Allen, Julia C., and Douglas F. Barnes. "The Causes of Deforestation in Developing Countries." *Annals of the Association of American Geographers* 75 no. 2(1985): 163–84.

Alston, Richard M. *The Individual vs. the Public Interest: Political Ideology and National Forest Policy*. Boulder, Colo.:Westview Press, 1985.

American Forest Products Industries. *Our Forest Bounty: Why We Must Have Multiple Use Forest Management*. Washington, D.C.: American Forest Products Industries, Inc., 1961.

Ames, J. D. "AIM Is Playing the Game—and Well." *Rapid City Journal,* 4 April 1982, p. 1.

———. "AIM to Sponsor Meeting of Tribes at Occupied Site." *Rapid City Journal,* 7 April 1981, p. 1.

———. "Bill Introduced to Set Aside 800 Hills Acres for Indian Use." *Rapid City Journal,* 4 March 1982, p. 1.

———. "Camp Dates Hills History to 1000 B.C." *Rapid City Journal,* 30 January 1985, p.1.

———. "Camp Tried to Usurp Power, Mathers Testifies." *Rapid City Journal,* 2 December 1982, pp. 1–2.

———. "FBI Turns Over File on Yellow Thunder Camp." *Rapid City Journal,* 1 December 1982, p. 2.

———. "Federal Law Requires Indian Role." *Rapid City Journal,* 31 January 1985, pp.1–2.

———. "Formidable Black Hills Battler Growing Tired of It All." *Rapid City Journal,* 7 March 1982, p. 23.

———. "Hines Plans to Sell Hill City Sawmill, Others." *Rapid City Journal,* 20 May 1982, p. 2.

———. "Historian Says the Black Hills Are Not a Sioux Holy Land." *Rapid City Journal,* 3 December, 1982, pp. 1–2.

147

————. "Historian Says Taking Hills Was Military Strategy." *Rapid City Journal*, 8 February 1985, pp. 1–2.

————."Homestake Strike Cripples Economy." *Rapid City Journal*, 1 August 1982, pp. 1–2.

————. "Homestake to Renew Mining in Open Cut." *Rapid City Journal*, 15 May 1985, p. 1.

————. "Independent Loggers in Financial Trouble." *Rapid City Journal*, 11 August 1980, p. 11.

————. "Indians Claim Black Hills land; Officials Planning Strategy." *Rapid City Journal*, 6 April 1981, pp. 1–2.

————. "Indians Settling In, Leaving Debris Behind." *Rapid City Journal*, 29 August 1981, p. 1.

————. "Judge Asked to Close Road to Yellow Thunder." *Rapid City Journal*, 19 August 1982, pp. 1–2.

————. "Lien Family Has Built an Empire on $100 and Some Rock." *Rapid City Journal*, 29 December 1980, p. 11.

————. "Local Mood Reflects Growing Racial Tensions." *Rapid City Journal*, 22 August 1982, pp. 1–2.

————. "Loggers Make Plight Public through Petition." *Rapid City Journal*, 8 July 1980, p. 1.

————. "Mathers Denies He Discriminated." *Rapid City Journal*, 10 February 1985, p. 1.

————. "Mathers Says Camp's Criticism Is Unfounded." *Rapid City Journal*, 10 May 1985, p. 1–2.

————. "Means Says Camp No Publicity Stunt." *Rapid City Journal*, 12 February 1985, p. 1.

————. "Mineral Wealth in State's Future?" *Rapid City Journal*, 6 December 1980, p. 1.

————. "Oral History Ties Lakota to Black Hills." *Rapid City Journal*, 1 February 1985, p. 1–2.

————. "Rancher Says U.S. Should Return Hills." *Rapid City Journal*, 24 March 1983, p. 2.

————. "Sawmills, Forest Service Split on Roundwood Policies." *Rapid City Journal*, 28 June 1982, p. 2.

————. "Southern Hills Citizens View Camp Warily." *Rapid City Journal*, 27 June 1981, pp. 1–2.

————. "Tollefson Shooting Introduced into Yellow Thunder Camp Trial." *Rapid City Journal*, 7 December 1982, p. 1–2.

————. "Victoria Occupation Stirs Indian Feelings." *Rapid City Journal*, 11 April 1981, p. 1–2.

————. "Witness Says Spiritual Guidance Led Lakota People to Black Hills." *Rapid City Journal*, 29 January 1985, pp. 1–2.

————. "Yellow Thunder Camp Trial Resumes." *Rapid City Journal*, 9 May 1985, pp. 1–2.

————. "Yellow Thunder Testimony Focuses on Religious Practice." *Rapid City Journal*, 30 November 1982, p. 1.

Anderson, Harry H. "An Account of Deadwood and the Northern Black Hills in 1876." *South Dakota Historical Collection*, no. 31 (1962):287–364.

"Another Wood Products Firm Moves into Sturgis." *Rapid City Journal,* 27 December 1978, p. 2.

"Anti-Wilderness Myths Dissolve Before Facts." *Rapid City Journal,* 23 April 1972, p. 44.

Ascher, William, and Robert Healy. *Natural Resource Policymaking in Developing Countries.* Durham, N.C.: Duke University Press, 1990.

Associate U.S. Solicitor. Legal Memorandum on Crazy Horse Monument. 13 December 1948. Custer, S.D.: Black Hills National Forest, Historic Files.

Averill, C. C. Letter to Pactola District re: individual mining claims. 14 September 1950. Custer, S.D.:Black Hills National Forest, Historic Files.

———. Letter to H. M. Huney re: cutting timber only for mining purposes. 1 May 1941. Custer, S.D.: Black Hills National Forest, Historic Files.

Baka, Ken. "AIM Leaders Charged with Illegal Tree Cutting." *Rapid City Journal,* 28 July 1983, p. 3.

———. "Ceremonial Fires Die as Sun Dancing Ends." *Rapid City Journal,* 22 July 1985, p. 1.

———. "Judge Lets Indians Remain at Camp." *Rapid City Journal,* 10 December 1985, p. 1.

———. "Most Tribes Want Land, Not Money in Treaty Disputes." *Rapid City Journal,* 14 March 1985, p. 1.

———. "Yellow Thunder Camp, Officials Reach Agreement on Sun Dance." *Rapid City Journal,* 12 July 1984, p. 3.

———. "Yellow Thunder Judge an Ethical 'Straight Arrow'." *Rapid City Journal,* 20 December 1985, sec. B, p. 1.

Baldwin, George P. *The Black Hills Illustrated.* Lead, S.D.: The Black Hills Mining Men's Association, 1904.

Bard, G. P. "Report on the Proposed Additions to and Eliminations from Sundance National Forest, Wyoming," submitted to U.S. Forest Service, July 1909. Custer, S.D.:Black Hills National Forest, Historic Files.

Barney, Daniel R. *The Last Stand.* New York: Grossman Publishers, 1974.

Batchelder, George A. "A Sketch of the History and Resources of Dakota Territory." *South Dakota Historical Collections* XIV (1928):181–252.

Beazley, Ronald. "Conservation Decision-making: A Rationalization." *Enclosing the Environment: NEPA's Transformation of Conservation into Environmentalism.* Edited by Channing Kury, 1–16 Albuquerque: University of New Mexico School of Law, 1985.

Bender, Ron. "Edgemont Unhappy with Outsiders' Views on Mining." *Rapid City Journal,* 12 March 1979, p. 1.

———. "Land Sales in Black Hills Are Increasing." *Rapid City Journal,* 23 February 1981, p. 11.

———. "Tourism Industry Puzzled by '84 Figures." *Rapid City Journal,* 13 January 1985, p. 2.

———. "Tourist Season Wasn't Nearly as Good as People Expected." *Rapid City Journal,* 31 August 1984, p. 2.

Bennett, John. *Northern Plainsman.* Chicago: Aldine Publishing Co., 1969.

Bjugstad, Ardell J. 1986. "Hybrid Poplar Cultivars for Maximizing Phytomass Production on Gold Mine Tailings in the Black Hills." *Proceedings of 1986 National*

Symposium on Mining, Hydrology, Sedimentology and Reclamation. 8–11 December 1986. Lexington, Ky: University of Kentucky.

———— Kenneth Kissel, and Walter Whitman. "Germination of Shrubs for Wildlife Habitat Restoration on Mined Lands in the Northern Great Plains." *Issues and Technology in the Management of Impacted Western Wildlife, Proceedings of a National Symposium.* Steamboat Springs, Colo, 15–17 November, 1982.

Black, Brad. "Black Elk Searches the Hills for Spirit of Departed Son." *Rapid City Journal,* 10 August 1949:1.

"Black Hills Forestry Yields More Wood than Area Started With." *Rapid City Journal,* 23 June 1968, p. 1.

"Black Hills National Forest Income Down." *Rapid City Journal,* 10 February 1899, p. 1.

Black Hills National Forest, Supervisor's Office. "Harney Peak 'Jeep' Trails Set for Closure." Press release. 6 May 1968. Custer, S.D. Black Hills National Forest, Historic Files.

"Black Hills Timber." *Rapid City Journal,* 10 February 1899, p.1.

Black Hills Trail Rides, Inc., and BHNF Forest Supervisor. "Agreement for Cooperative Work." 10 December 1971. Custer, S.D.:Black Hills National Forest Historic Files.

Blackmer, Stephen D. "Whose Woods Are These . . . The Future of New England's Forests." *The Environmental Forum* Nov./Dec.(1988):19–21.

Blahna, Dale J. "Social Bases for Resource Conflicts in Areas of Reverse Migration." Edited by Robert G. Lee, Donald R. Field, and William R. Burch, *Community and Forestry.* (Boulder, Colo: Westview Press 1990) 159–78.

Blaikie, Piers, and Harold Brookfield. *Land Degradation and Society.* London: Methuen, 1987.

Bock, Carl E., and Jane H. Bock. "Responses of Birds and Deer Mice to Prescribed Burning in Ponderosa Pine." *Journal of Wildlife Management* 47.3 (1983):837–40.

Boerker, Richard H. D. *Our National Forests.* New York: The Macmillan Company, 1920.

Boldt, Charles E. Memorandum to U.S.Forest Service re: research value of Upper Pine Creek. 10 March 1966. Custer, S.D.: Black Hills National Forest Historic Files.

————. *Shelterwoods in Black Hills Ponderosa Pine.* Proceedings of the National Silviculture Workshop 17–21 September 1979. Charleston, S.C.

————. *Sequential Thinnings Boost Productivity of a Ponderosa Pine Stand in the Black Hills of South Dakota.* U.S.Department of Agriculture Forest Service Research Note RM-172. Fort Collins, Colo.: Rocky Mountain Forest and Range Experiment Station, 1970.

———— and James L. Van Deusen. *Silviculture of Ponderosa Pine in the Black Hills: The status of our knowledge.* U.S.Department of Agriculture Forest Service Research Paper RM-124. Fort Collins,Colo:Rocky Mountain Forest and Range Experiment Station, 1974.

Bowes, Michael D., and John V. Krutilla. *Multiple-Use Management: The Economics of Public Forestlands.* Washington, D.C.: Resources for the Future, 1989.

Bradbury, Ray. "Gold Miners Destroying Streams, Says GF&P." *Rapid City Journal,* 17 September 1982, p. 2.

————. "Homestake Must Keep Paying Severance Tax." *Rapid City Journal,* 22 August 1983. p. 1.

————. "Miner Wins Over Game, Fish, and Parks." *Rapid City Journal* 21 May 1982. p. 2.

————. "Witness Expenses Dispute Could Delay Trial." *Rapid City Journal* 24 November 1982, p. 1–2.

————. "Yellow Thunder Camp Trial Under Way in Pierre." *Rapid City Journal,* 22 November 1982, p. 1–2.

Bradley, Harold C. Letter to Regional Forester complaining about Crazy Horse Monument. 29 April 1949. Custer, S.D.,Black Hills National Forest Historic Files.

————. Letter to Secretary of Agriculture complaining about Crazy Horse Monument. 16 June 1949. Custer, S.D.: Black Hills National Forest Historic File.

Brademeyer, Brad. Personal Interview. 11 November 1992.

Briggs, Harold E. "Ranching and Stock-raising in the Territory of Dakota." *South Dakota Historical Collections* XIV (1928):417–66.

Brokaw, Chet. "Trout Thriving in Creek Given New Life by Mining Company." *Rapid City Journal,* 14 November 1985, sec. D. p. 1.

Bromley, Daniel W., and Michael M. Cernea. *The Management of Common Property Resources.* Washington, D.C.: The World Bank [World Bank Discussion Paper No.57], 1989.

Brown, Dee. *Bury My Heart at Wounded Knee: An Indian History of the American West.* New York: Holt, Rinehart, and Winston, 1970.

Brown, Marguerite. "Elk Mountain Proposals Reviewed at Newcastle." *Rapid City Journal,* 1 April 1972.

Brubaker, Sterling, ed. *Rethinking the Federal Lands.* Washington, D.C: Resources for the Future, 1984.

Bruce, John W. and Louise Fortmann. "Why Land Tenure and Tree Tenure Matter: Some Fuel for Thought." Edited by Louise Fortmann, and John W. Bruce, 1–10. *Whose Trees? Proprietary Dimensions of Forestry.* Boulder, Colo: Westview Press, 1988.

Buck, Susan. "Cultural Theory and Management of Common Property Resources," *Human Ecology* 17(1989):101–16.

Burke, Florence. *Silver City: One Hundred Years of Black Hills History, 1876–1976.* Silver City, S.D.: Historical Society, 1977.

Burke, Joseph P. Letter to Forest Service re: timber permit on mining claim. 21 June 1941. Custer, S.D.:Black Hills National Forest Historic Files.

Burlington Route. *The Black Hills Detour.* Chicago: Burlington Route Passenger Department, 1935.

Cannon, Jack. "Forest Has Role in History." *Rapid City Journal,* 12 March 1961, p. 25.

————. "Hills Water Problems Discussed-No Solution." *Rapid City Journal,* 19 October 1954, pp. 1,4.

————. "'Operation Outdoors' Now in Progress." *Rapid City Journal,* 13 October 1957, p. 19.

Carson, Rachel. *Silent Spring.* Boston, Mass: Houghton- Mifflin,1962.

Carter, E. E. Letter to H. Huney re: mining claim/timber cutting rules. 24 June 1941. Custer, S.D.: Black Hills National Forest Historic Files.

Cassells, E.Steven, David B. Miller, and Paul V. Miller. *Paha Sapa: A Cultural Resource Overview of the Black Hills National Forest, South Dakota and Wyoming.* Longmont, Colo.: Plano Archeological Consultants, 1984.

"Cattle vs. Sheep." *Rapid City Journal,* 21 September 1898, p. 1.

Cawley, R. McGreggor. *Federal Land, Western Anger: The Sagebrush Rebellion and Environmental Politics.* Lawrence: University Press of Kansas, 1993.

Chevance, Norman. "Cultural Resources Survey in the Driftwood Canyon and Long Mountain Regions, Fall River County." Report to U.S.Forest Service, Custer, SD, 1979.

Chicago and NorthWestern Railway. *The Black Hills South Dakota, The Richest Hundred Miles Square in the World.* Chicago: Chicago and NorthWestern Railway, 1916.

———. *Green "Gold" in the Black Hills: A Survey of the Pulpwood Potential of the Black Hills Pondersosa Pine.* Chicago: Chicago and NorthWestern Railway, 1955.

———. *A Guide to the Black Hills Sawmills and Wood Products Industries in Chicago and NorthWestern Railway Territory.* Chicago: Chicago and NorthWestern Railway, 1955.

———. *Lumber Manufacturing Possibilities in the Black Hills.* Chicago: Chicago and NorthWestern Railway, 1956.

———. *The Pulpwood Resources of the Black Hills.* Chicago: Chicago and NorthWestern Railway, 1956.

———. *Pulpwood: A Study of the Wood Fiber Resources of the Black Hills and Wyoming Tributary to the Chicago and NorthWestern Railway.* Chicago: Chicago and NorthWestern Railway Company, 1964.

Clark, W. R., and J. R. Medcraft. "Wildlife Use of Shrubs on Reclaimed Surface-mined Land in Northeastern Wyoming." *Journal of Wildlife Management* 50.4 (1986): 714–18.

Clawson, Marion. "Conflicts, Strategies, and Possibilities for Consensus in Forest Land Use and Management." Proceedings of Conference on Forest Policy for the Future. 8–9 May, 1974. Washington, D.C: Resources for the Future, 1974.

———. *The Federal Lands Revisited.* Washington, D.C.: Resources for the Future, 1983.

———. *Forests For Whom and For What?* Baltimore: The Johns Hopkins University Press for Resources for the Future, 1975.

———, and Burnell Held. *The Federal Lands: Their Use and Management.* Baltimore: The Johns Hopkins University Press for Resources for the Future, 1957.

Conner, John. Letter to U.S. Forest Service Ranger requesting investigation of vandalism at Jewel Cave. 12 November 1923. Custer, S.D. Black Hills National Forest Historic Files.

———. Letter to Supervisor, Harney National Forest, complaining about Jewel Cave being locked. 30 December 1926. Custer, S.D.: Black Hills National Forest Historic Files.

Connolly, Joseph P., and Cleophas C. O'Harra. *The Mineral Wealth of the Black Hills.* Rapid City, S.D.: South Dakota School of Mines (Bulletin No. 16), 1929.

Cosgrove, Dennis. "Landscape and Social Formation: Theoretical Considerations." *Social Formation and Symbolic Landscape.* Totowa, N.J.: Barnes and Noble, 1984.

Coursey, O. W. *Beautiful Black Hills: A Comprehensive Treatise on the Black Hills of South Dakota, Non-Technical for Popular Reading.* Mitchell, S.D.: Educator Supply Co., 1926.

Crawford, Lewis F. *The Medora-Deadwood Stage Line.* Bismark, N.D.: Capital Book Co., 1925.

Cruse, James C. *Effects on Wildlife of the Proposed Harney Peak Aerial Tramway Development*. Custer, S.D.: Black Hills National Forest Historic Files. 1970.

Culhane, Paul J. *Public Lands Politics*. Baltimore: The Johns Hopkins University Press for Resources for the Future, 1981.

Custer Commercial Club. Letter to Senator Peter Norbeck asking for a Senate Appropriation to buy Jewel Cave mining claims. 12 November 1923. Custer: S.D.: Black Hills National Forest Historic File.

Custer County (S.D.). *Comprehensive Plan, Custer County, South Dakota, 1972.*

Custer County Centennial Committee. *A Brief History of Custer County, South Dakota.* Custer, S.D.: Custer County Centennial Committee, 1961.

Cutschall, Maureen. "Supporters Claim Archeological Sites Prove Lakota Culture in Hills." *Rapid City Journal,* 29 June 1982, p. 1.

Daly, Bob. "Visitors Bureau Cites Post-Flood Efforts: Mount Rushmore Security Warning Issued." *Rapid City Journal,* 21 March 1973, p. 3.

Danzger, D. H. 1975. "Validating Conflict Data." *The American Sociological Review* 40:570–84.

Darrow, Corrine. Personal Interview. 10 November 1992.

Davis, B. L., D. N. Blair, L. R. Johnson, and S. L. Haggard. "A Study of the Green Area Effect in the Black Hills of South Dakota." *Atmospheric Environment* 10(1976): 363–70.

Davis, Lauren. "Area Mineral Development Presents Two-Sided Coin." *Rapid City Journal,* 23 September 1977, p. 1.

Deacon, Robert T., and M. Bruce Johnson. "Introduction." Edited by Robert T. Deacon and M. Bruce Johnson. *Forestlands.* San Fransciso: Pacific Institute for Public Policy, 1985.

DeWitt, E., J. A. Redden, D. Buscher and A. B. Wilson. *Geologic Map of the Black Hills Area, South Dakota and Wyoming.* Washington, D.C.: U.S. Geological Survey, 1989.

Dietz, D. R. and J. R. Tigner. "Evaluation of Two Mammal Repellents Applied to Browse Species in the Black Hills." *The Journal of Wildlife Management* 32.1 (1968):109–111.

Dietz, D. R., Daniel W. Uresk, H. E. Messner, and L.C. McEwen. *Establishment, Survival and Growth of Selected Browse Species in a Ponderosa Pine Forest.* USDA Forest Service Research Paper RM-219. Fort Collins, Colo: Rocky Mountain Forest and Range Experiment Station, 1980.

Distad, Arnold O. *The Development of Transportation Facilities in Lawrence and Pennington Counties, 1876–1936.* Vermillion: University of South Dakota, 1940.

Donnelly, D. M., and H. E. Worth. *Potential for Producing Ponderosa Pine Plywood in the Black Hills.* Rapid City: USDA Forest Service, Rocky Mountain Forest and Range Experiment Station, 1981.

"Dramatic New Management Concept for Forests Started in Hills." *Rapid City Journal,* 20 February 1972, p. 1.

Duncan, John, and Nancy Duncan. "(Re)reading the Landscape." *Environment and Planning D: Society and Space* 6(1988): 117–26.

Driscoll, R. E. *Seventy Years of Banking in the Black Hills.* Rapid City, S.D.: The Gate City Guide, 1948.

Duthie, George A. "Plan for Handling the Timber Business of the Black Hills and Harney Forests". undated (circa 1952). Custer, S.D.: Black Hills National Forest

Historic Files.

———. "Timber, An Economic Resource of the Black Hills." *The Black Hills Engineer* 16.2(1928): 101–9.

Dysart, Benjamin C., and Marion Clawson. *Managing Public Lands in the Public Interest*. New York: Praeger, 1988.

Edgington, Dick. "Hell's Angels Set USA Run near Custer." *Rapid City Journal,* 23 June 1983, pp. 1,2.

Edwards, G. D. *Preliminary Report of Recreational Use and Development, Deerfield Reservoir Site on Castle Creek Pennington County, South Dakota*. Billings, Mont.: National Park Service, 1947.

Egner, Dick. "Indian Group to Ask for 3.2 Million Acres in Hills." *Rapid City Journal,* 29 June 1982, p. 1.

———. "Indians to Reintroduce Camp Bill in January." *Rapid City Journal,* 12 December 1982, p. 2.

———. "Religion a Big Part of Daily Life at Yellow Thunder, Means Says." *Rapid City Journal,* 5 December 1982, p. 1.

Ellis, David, M.(ed). *Frontiers in American Development*. Ithaca: Cornell University Press. 1969.

Emel, Jacque, and Richard Peet. "Resource Management and Natural Hazards." Edited by Richard Peet and Nigel Thrift, 49–76. *New Models in Geography: The Political Economy Perspective*. London: Unwin Hyman, 1989.

Erickson, Ken. "Senate Approves Measures to Stem Air, Water Pollution Originating from Homestake Mine." *Rapid City Journal,* 28 January 1976, p. 2.

Evans, E. *Conservation of South Dakota's Natural Resources*. Pierre, S.D.: State Publishing Co., 1953.

Fall River County Historical Society. *Fall River County Pioneer Histories*. Hot Springs, S.D.: Fall River County Historical Society, 1976.

Farrar, Sharon. "Hills Water Sports Due to Farmers' Efforts." *Rapid City Journal,* 11 November 1976, p. 6.

"Farewell to President Cleveland." *Rapid City Journal,* 4 March 1897, p. 1.

Fast Horse, Charles T. "Special Use Application (Yellow Thunder Camp) to USFS," Custer, S.D. 3 March 1979.

———. "Notice of Appeal to USFS." 27 November 1979. Custer, S.D. Black Hills National Forest Historic Files.

Fick, Bob. "Forest Management Plan Draws Criticism." *Rapid City Journal,* 11 March 1982, p. 2.

Fielder, Mildred. *Railroads of the Black Hills*. Deadwood, S.D.: Dakota Graphics, 1985.

Fincher, Ruth. "The Political Economy of the Local State." Edited by Richard Peet and Nigel Thrift, 338–60, *New Models in Geography: The Political Economy Perspective*. London: Unwin, Hyman, 1989.

Fite, Gilbert. *Mount Rushmore*. Norman: University of Oklahoma Press, 1952.

"Forest Reserve Set Aside." *Rapid City Journal,* 9 May 1897, p. 1.

"Foresters' Views of Interest Group Positions on Forest Policy." *Journal of Forestry,* June (1972):337–42.

"Forests Merge." *Rapid City Journal,* 7 February 1954, p. 20.

Fortmann, Louise, and Bruce, John W. *Whose Trees: Proprietary Dimensions of*

Forestry. Boulder, Colo.: Westview Press, 1988.

Frantz, Anne C. "Tourism in Area Ranged from 'Mediocre' to 'Wonderful'." *Rapid City Journal,* 18 September 1985.

———. "Traveling Writers Focus on Hills Area Tackiness." *Rapid City Journal,* 7 September 1985, p. 11.

Franzosi, R. 1987. "The press as a source of socio-historical data: Issues in the methodology of data collection from newspapers." *Historical Methods* 20(1): 5–6.

Freed, Diane. "Sioux Consider Black Hills a Battle a Religious Cause." *Rocky Mountain News,* 28 September 1980, p. 4.

Fritch, D. Letter re: Sheridan Lake 10 day permits to USFS, Custer. 24 March 1980. Custer, S.D.: BHNF, Historic Files.

Froiland, Steven G. *Natural History of the Black Hills and Badlands.* Sioux Falls, S.D.: The Center for Western Studies, 1990.

Frome, Michael. *The Forest Service.* Boulder, Colo.: Westview Press, 1984.

"Full of Meat." *Rapid City Journal,* 11 December, 1897, p. 1.

"A Fundamental Problem of the Black Hills National Forest." *South Dakota Conservation Digest* Jan./Feb.(1957):2–4.

Gardner, Roy, Elinor Ostrom, James M. Walker. "The Nature of Common Pool Resource Problems" *Rationality and Society* 2.3 (1990):335–58.

Garrison, G. A., A. J.Bjugstad, D. A.Duncan, M. E.Lewis, and D. R.Smith. *Vegetation and Environmental Features of Forest and Range Ecosystems.* Government Printing Office: Washington, D.C. Agriculture Handbook No. 475, 1977.

Gartner, F. R., and Kieth E. Severson. "Fee Hunting in Western South Dakota." *Journal of Range Management* 25.3 (1972): 234–7.

Gebhart, Tim. "'Finally Home' is Wind Cave Message." *Rapid City Journal,* 26 June 1981, p. 2.

———. "Gold Tax Bill Could Net State $7.6 Million." *Rapid City Journal,* 28 February 1981, p. 1.

———. "Indian Dream Could Become White Man's Real Nightmare." *Rapid City Journal,* 7 September 1980, p. 2.

———. "Indians to File Suit Against Mathers, Janklow". *Rapid City Journal,* 24 November 1981, p. 2.

———. "Tribe May Appeal Ruling on Homestake Suit." *Rapid City Journal,* 14 August 1982, p. 2.

Getz, Jack. "Discussions Continue on Fires at Sun Dance." *Rapid City Journal,* 19 July 1985, p. 1.

———. "Forest Service Chief Sees 'Great Future' for Hills." *Rapid City Journal,* 17 August 1976, p. 9.

———. "Logging Activity in the Black Hills May Grow if Market Can Be Found." *Rapid City Journal,* 5 February 1977, p. 13.

"GF&P Drops Sheridan Lake Fish Proposals." *Rapid City Journal,* 29 March 1973, p. 1,2.

Ginter, P. L. "The Influence of the Small Sawmill on the Prosperity of the Black Hills." 16.2 (1928): 110–16. *The Black Hills Engineer.*

Gladstone, Lynn. "Black Hawk Residents Assured of Hearing on Surface Mining Permit." *Rapid City Journal,* 11 October 1975, p. 2.

———. "Black Hills Dam Standards Raised Since 1972 Flood." *Rapid City Journal,*

15 November 1977p. 1.

———. "Black Hills Lumber Mills Expanding Toward East." *Rapid City Journal,* 26 August 1978, p. 5.

———. "Ending Pollution Cost Homestake $14 Million." *Rapid City Journal,* 22 September 1978, p. 14.

———. "Forest Management Practices Urged for Inclusion in Water Quality Plan." *Rapid City Journal,* 9 June 1977, p. 3.

———. "Forest Service Impartial on Roadless Area Issue." *Rapid City Journal,* 7 July 1978, p. 2.

———. "Grass Doing Well on Quarried Land." *Rapid City Journal,* 24 June 1977, p. 9.

———. "Homestake to Pay $390,000 Pollution Penalty." *Rapid City Journal,* 8 February 1980, 2.

———. "Homestake to Spend $10 Million in Cleanup." *Rapid City Journal,* 20 May 1976, p. 1.

———. "Homestake to Spend $12.1 Million to Comply with Pollution Standards." *Rapid City Journal,* 14 November 1976, p. 3.

———. "Pegmatite-'Promising, Exciting.'" *Rapid City Journal,* 20 March 1977, p. 25.

———. "Polluted Creek Now Runs Clear." *Rapid City Journal* 27 August 1978:29.

———. "Projected Influx of Tourists During 1976 Poses Some Problems for Forest Service." *Rapid City Journal,* 2 April 1976, p. 2.

———. "Surface Mining and Regulations Discussed at Mining Workshop." *Rapid City Journal,* 14 March 1975, p. 2.

———. "Timbering Affected by Labor, Set-Aside." *Rapid City Journal,* 18 February 1978, Sec. S, p. 5.

———. "Tourism Hit Unexpected High." *Rapid City Journal,* 6 January 1977, p. 1.

———. "Uranium Mining Expected to Put New Pressure on Elk Mountain District." *Rapid City Journal,* 9 December 1978, p. 16.

———. "Uranium Mining Area Set to Begin in 1980." *Rapid City Journal,* 29 November 1978, p. 1,2.

———. "Use Now Being Made of Sawmill Waste Products". *Rapid City Journal,* 20 November 1978, p. 2.

———. "Whitewood Lumber Plant Diversifying." *Rapid City Journal,* 21 November 1978, p. 2.

Glemens, Donald E., and Daniel F. Burroughs. *Missouri River Basin Survey.* Billings, Mont.: National Park Service, 1956.

"Good News for the Hills." *Rapid City Journal,* 9 July 1898, p. 1.

Goss, Sidney G., Robert T. Wagner, and Robert M. Dimit. *Population Change in South Dakota Small Towns: 1960- 1970.* Brookings,S.D.: Agricultural Experiment Station, South Dakota State University (Bulletin 636, 1970 Population Review Series No.9), 1975.

Gray, W. K., A. A. Volk, A. M. Dreyer, M. L. White, and V. E. Montgomery. *South Dakota Economic and Business Abstract.* Vermillion: University of South Dakota, 1963.

Green, Charles L. "The Administration of the Public Domain in South Dakota." *South Dakota Historical Collections.* Pierre, S.D.: Hipple Publishing Co., 1940.

"Group Expresses Its Opposition to Hills Claim, Spiritual Camp." *Rapid City Journal,* 14 June 1979, p. 6.

Guayle, Plesser, and Co., Inc. "Black Hills Values Survey." Report prepared for Sixth District Council of Local Governments, Rapid City, S.D., 1975.

Gulbranson, John. "Forest Service Digging into Ancient History at Site near Edgemont." *Rapid City Journal,* 6 November 1977, p. 3.

———. "Weston County Has Dual Economic Base." *Rapid City Journal,* 29 February 1976, p. 21.

Hall, George. "The Myth and Reality of Multiple Use Forestry." *Natural Resources Journal* 3 (1963):276–90.

Hamner, Greene, and Siler Associates. *Economy of the Sixth Planning and Development District of South Dakota.* Pierre, S.D.: Economic and Development Council, 1973.

Hanson, Gordon. "Aerial Tram Is Unique." *Rapid City Journal,* 26 May 1963, p. 1.

———. "People Near Camp against Proposal." *Rapid City Journal,* 24 November 1984, p. 1,2.

Hardin, Garrett. "The Tragedy of the Commons." *Science* 162:1243–48, 1968.

———. and J. Baden. *Managing the Commons.* San Francisco: W.H. Freeman & Co., 1977.

Harding, Del. Letter to James Mathers (Forest Supervisor) re: USFS reactions to Fast Horse special use application. June 5, 1979.

Harlan, Bob. "Hills Economy Still Dominated by 'The Big Three,' Study Shows." *Rapid City Journal* 25 March 1985:1.

———. "Property Owners Oppose Mixing Mining, Skiing." *Rapid City Journal* 22 December 1985:A-2.

Harney Forest Supervisor. Letter to District Forest Supervisor re: Jewel Cave mining claim. May 6,1919. Black Hills National Forest Historic Files, Custer.

Harris, Cole. "The Historical Mind and the Practice of Geography." Eds. David Ley and Marwyn S. Samuels. *Humanistic Geography: Prospects and Problems.* London: Croom Helm, 1978.

Hawkes, C.L. and L.A. Norris. "Chronic Oral Toxicity of 2, 3, 7, 8-Tetrachlorodibenzo-p-dioxin (TCCD) to Rainbow Trout." *Transactions of the American Fisheries Society* 106.6 (1977): 641–45.

Heaberlin, Tina. "Taconite Mining near Nemo, Coal Mining in Wyoming Highlight Discussion." *Rapid City Journal* 17 January 1975:2.

Hecht, Susanna. "Environment, Development and Politics: Capital Accumulation and the Livestock Sector in Eastern Amazonia." *World Development* 13.6 (1985): 663–85.

"Hill City Economy." *Rapid City Journal* February 2, 1899:1.

Hill, Bill. "Wilderness Issue Is a Continuing Controversy." *Rapid City Journal* 22 April 1979:2.

Hoffman, G.R. and R.R. Alexander. *Forest Vegetation of the Black Hills National Forest of South Dakota and Wyoming: A Habitat Type Classification.* USDA Forest Service Research Paper RM-276. Fort Collins, CO: Rocky Mountain Forest and Range Experiment Station, 1987.

Hogan, Edward P. *The Reasons for Out-Migration of South Dakota Youth.* Ann Arbor: University Microfilms, 1970.

Hood, A.B. "Logging Operations in the Black Hills." *The Black Hills Engineer* 16.2 (1928):120–135.

Hoover, Herbert T. 1984. "Some Recommended Sources on South Dakota History and

Culture." Edited Herbert T.Hoover, pp.3–7. *Planning for the South Dakota Centennial: A Bibliography.* Brookings, SD: University of South Dakota, 1984.

Howe, M. and D. Noble. 1985. "Effect of Cyanide Residue on Vegetation Bordering a Black Hills Stream." *Proceedings of the South Dakota Academy of Sciences* 64:112–22.

Hudson, John C. *Plains Country Towns.* Minneapolis: University of Minnesota Press, 1983.

Huney, Hazel. Letter to President Roosevelt re: mining claim in BHNF. 12 June 1941. Custer, S.D.: Black Hills National Forest, Historic Files.

———. Letter to District Ranger re: timber policy. 10 May 1941. Custer, S.D.: Black Hills National Forest, Historic Files.

Hyde, M. B. Letter to Senator Mundt re: opposition to Harney Peak development. 16 May 1970. Custer, S.D.:Black Hills National Forest, Historic Files.

Imrie, Bob. "Custer Wants to Dump Wastewater in Creek; Some Landowners Object." *Rapid City Journal,* 5 January 1984, p. 1.

———. "Disgruntled Sturgis Citizens Rally Support for End to Bike Classic." *Rapid City Journal,* 24 August 1982, p. 1.

———. "Fire at Sawmill Was Final Blow." *Rapid City Journal,* 15 May 1980, pp. 1,2.

———. "Sturgis Council Hears from the People on Rally". *Rapid City Journal,* 17 August 1982, pp 1,2.

———. "Supreme Court Rules Homestake Is Not Entitled to Gold Tax Refund." *Rapid City Journal,* 6 September 1985, p. 2

"Indian Retreat Site Opposed by Landowners." *Rapid City Journal,* 24 April 1979, p 1.

"Indian Spiritual Site Requested." *Custer County Chronicle,* 26 April 1979, p.1.

"Indians Hold Cattle for Ransom." *Rapid City Journal,* 26 May 1897, p. 1.

Ingvalsen, F.L. Letter to Howard Lee. 16 February 1961. Custer, S.D.: Black Hills National Forest Historic Files.

Ivins, Meredeth. "'Outsiders' Blamed for Wyoming's Growing Pains." *Rapid City Journal,* 24 April 1978, p. 1.

Jackson, J. B. *Discovering the Vernacular Landscape.* New Haven, Conn.: Yale University Press, 1984.

Jackson, Henry. "Environmental Policy and the Congress." Edited by Channing Kury, 36–57 *Enclosing the Environment: NEPA's Transformation of Conservation into Environmentalism.* Albuquerque, N.M.: University of New Mexico, 1985.

"Jewel Cave." *Rapid City Journal,* 16 March 1964, p. 1.

"Job Involves Protecting Forest's Cultural Resources." *Rapid City Journal,* 6 November 1977, p. 1.

Johansen, John P. *Population trends in relation to resources development in South Dakota.* Brookings, S.D.: Agricultural Experiment Station, South Dakota State University, 1954.

Johnson, A. I. "The Mining Industry in South Dakota." *The Black Hills Engineer.* 26.1 (1940):50–59.

Johnson, George. "Indians Join Uranium Protest." *Rapid City Journal,* 8 June 1981, pp. 1,2.

———. "State Reneged on Roads, Say Residents." *Rapid City Journal,* 20 November 1981, p. 2.

Johnson, Robert H. "U.S. Forest Service and Its Budget." *Forestlands.* (San Francisco:

Pacific Institute for Public Policy Research, 1985) 103–134.

Jones, Lilias. "A History of the Black Hills." *Keystone to Survival: The Multinational Corporations and the Struggle for Control of Land.* Rapid City, S.D.:Black Hills Alliance, 1981.

Junge, Mark. "Historic Inyan Kara." *Bits and Pieces* 8.5(1972):1–9.

Karsten, A. "South Dakota Natural Resources or Raw Materials and their Industrialization." *The Black Hills Engineer* 26.1 (1940):3–39.

Kelleher, Peter D. "The National Forests of the Black Hills." *Pahasapa Quarterly* 2.4 (1913):9–12.

———. "The Tourist in the Black Hills." *Pahasapa Quarterly* 10 (1921):194–8.

Kern, John C. Letter to Bureau of Reclamation re permits to be affected by Pactola Reservoir. 18 February 1955. Custer, S.D.:Black Hills National Forest Historic Files.

———. Letter to Regional Forester re Pactola Reservoir. 12 July, 1955. Custer, S.D.: Black Hills National Forest Historic Files.

Kessler, Dick. Personal Interview. 10 November 1992.

Kravig, M. C. Letter to Secretary Hardin re: opposition to Harney Peak development. 6 May 1970. Custer, S.D.:Black Hills National Forest,Historic Files.

Krutilla, John V., Michael D. Bowes and Elizabeth A. Wilman. "National Forest System Planning and Management: An Analytical Review and Suggested Approach." Edited by Roger A.Sedjo, 207–36. *Governmental Interventions, Social Needs, and the Management of U.S. Forests.* Washington, D.C.: Resources for the Future, 1983.

Kury, Channing. *Enclosing the Environment: NEPA's Transformation of Conservation into Environmentalism.* Albuquerque: University of New Mexico School of Law, 1985.

LaFoone, P.C. Letter to Forest Service re: opposition to Harney Peak development. 6 April 1970. Custer, S.D.:Black Hills National Forest Historic Files.

"Largest Sale in Hills History Made." *Hill City Prevailer,* 9 October 1980, p.1.

Laughlin, Charles J. "Ponderosa Pine-A Valuable Source of Raw Material." *The Black Hills Engineer* 26.1 (1940):39–46.

Lazarus, Edward. *Black Hills White Justice.* New York: Harper Collins, 1991.

Lee, Bob. "Every Resident Owes $1,000 to the Sioux as Payment for Black Hills." *Rapid City Journal,* 4 October 1948, p.16.

Lee, F.S. Letter to Regional Forester supporting airport for Custer. 19 October 1960. Custer, S.D.: Black Hills National Forest, Historic Files.

Lee, Robert. "Bentonite Edges Gold in State in Precious Mineral Resources." *Rapid City Journal,* 22 November 1965, p. 2.

———. "Mineral Production in State Again Filling Industry Needs." *Rapid City Journal,* 13 November 1965, p. 10.

Lee, Robert G. "Sustained Yield and Social Order." Edited by Robert G.Lee, Donald R. Field and J.William Burch, 83-95. *Community and Forestry.* Boulder, Colo: Westview Press, 1990.

Leete, B. E. "The National Forests of the Black Hills." *Pahasapa Quarterly* 9(1920): 191–99.

Leisz, Douglas R. "Impacts of the RPA/NMFA Planning Process on Management and Planning in the Forest Service." Edited by Roger A. Sedjo, 245–57. *Governmental Interventions, Social Needs, and the Management of U.S. Forests.* Washington,

D.C.: Resources for the Future, 1983.

Leonard, H. Jeffrey. *Natural Resource Use and Economic Development in Central America*. Washington, D.C.: International Institute for Environment and Development, 1987.

Levenson, Bill. "Forest Service, OMB at Odds Over Forest Management Responsibility." *Rapid City Journal*, 29 December 1979, p. 2.

Ley, David. "Social Geography and the Taken-For-Granted World." *Transactions, Institute of British Geographers* 2 (1977): 498–512.

Lincoln, Francis C. 1937. "Mining in South Dakota." Edited by Francis C.Lincoln, Walter G. Miser and Joseph B. Cummings, 10–43. *The Mining Industry of South Dakota*. Bulletin No. 17. Rapid City, S.D.: South Dakota School of Mines, 1937.

Linde, Martha. *Sawmills of the Black Hills*. Rapid City,S.D.: Jessie Y. Sundstrom, 1984.

Lively, J. "Firm Still Pumping Cyanide-Tainted Water from Ponds at Mine by Lead." *Rapid City Journal*, 19 June 1984, p. 2.

"Logging History." *Rapid City Journal*, 13 June 1968, p. 1.

Long, Larry. *Migration and Residential Mobility in the United States*. New York: Russell Sage Foundation, 1988.

Lowenthal, David. "The Place of the Past in the American Landscape." Edited by David Lowenthal and Martyn Bowden. *Geographies of the Mind*, 1976.

Lynn, Arthur. "A Report of Timber Conditions and Sales Procedures on the Black Hills National Forest." Custer, S.D., Black Hills National Forest, Historic Files, 1960.

Mader, Marie. "Sheridan Lake Users Find Fees Unfair." *Rapid City Journal*, 1 July 1984, p. 1.

Markstrom, Donald C. and David H. Clark. "Service Life of Treated and Untreated Black Hills Ponderosa Pine Fenceposts: A Progress Report". USDA Forest Service Research Note RM-303. Fort Collins, Colo.: Rocky Mountain Forest and Range Experiment Station, 1975.

———, William F. Lehmann, and J. Dobbin McNatt. "Technical Feasibility of Producing Particileboard from Black Hills Ponderosa Pine." USDA Forest Service Research Paper RM-173. Fort Collins, Colo.: Rocky Mountain Forest And Range Experiment Station, 1976.

——— and Harold E. Worth. *Economic Potentials for Particleboard Production in the Black Hills*. Rapid City, S.D.: USDA Rocky Mountain Forest and Range Experiment Station, 1981.

———, H. E. Troxell, and C. E. Boldt. "Wood Properties of Immature Ponderosa Pine After Thinning." *Forest Products Journal* 33.4 (1983):33–36.

Martens, H. H., E. Bailey, and R. Leonhardt. *History of Soil and Water Conservation Districts*. Brookings,S.D.: South Dakota Association of Soil and Water Conservations Districts, 1969.

Martin, Philip. "Conflict Resolution through the Multiple-Use Concept in Forest Service Decision-Making." *Natural Resources Journal* 9 (1969): 228–36.

Mathers, James R. Environmental Assessment Report on Lakota Camp. 13 July 1979. Custer, S.D.: Black Hills National Forest Historic Files.

———. "Forest Service Outlines How Resources Are Managed." *Rapid City Journal*, 16 November 1985, sec.C, p. 3.

———. Letter to Riley re: Official response to Lakota Request. 21 September 1979.

Custer, S.D.:Black Hills National Forest Historic Files.

————. "Year in Review." *Rapid City Journal,* 31 December 1984, p. 2.

McArdle, Richard E. Letter to Administrator, Bureau of Land Management re: Land exchange for Crazy Horse Monument. 17 June 1953. Custer, S.D.: Black Hills National Forest Historic Files.

McCay, Bonnie J., and James M. Acheson. *The Question of the Commons: The Culture and Ecology of Communal Resources.* Tucson, Ariz.: The University of Arizona Press, 1987.

McConnell, Grant. "The Conservation Movement — Past and Present." *The Western Political Quarterly* 7(1954):463–78.

McGovern, George. "A Bill to Designate Certain Lands in the Black Hills National Forest, South Dakota as the Black Elk Wilderness." *Congressional Record,* 18 September 1979: S12893; and 25 September 1980: S13477 and S13476.

McKean, Margaret and Elinor Ostrom. "Common Property Regimes in the Forest: Just a Relic from the Past?" *Unasylva180* 46(1995).

Means, Bill. "The History of the Lakota People." *Keystone to Survival: Multinational Corporations and the Struggle for Control of Land.* Rapid City, S.D.: Black Hills Alliance, 1981.

Means, Russell. "The Western Mind: An Indian Point of View." *Keystone to Survival: The Multinational Corporations and the Struggle for Control of Land.* Rapid City, S.D.: Black Hills Alliance, 1981.

Meinig, Donald, M. *Interpretation of Ordinary Landscapes.* Oxford: Oxford University Press, 1979.

Melle, A. Letter to R. Lynn re: cooperation with Custer State Forest. 28 May 1980. Custer, S.D., Black Hills National Forest Historic Files, Custer.

Mercer, Bob. "South Dakota Wants a Piece of the Rock." *Washington Post,* 4 July 1995, sec. A, p. 8.

Michaud, Frank. Letter re: Jewel Cave to Smith Riley, District Forester. 26 October 1919. Custer, S.D.: Black Hills National Forest Historic Files.

Milhans, Bruce. "Cattle Ear Tags to Aid Grazing Management." *Rapid City Journal,* 21 March 1983, p. 2.

————. "Custer Residents Complain Mill Is Too Noisy, Pollutes Air." *Rapid City Journal,* 15 May 1983, p. 13.

————. "Forest Service Officer Clarifies Forest Sale Study." *Rapid City Journal,* 15 June 1983, p. 3.

————. "Grazing Cattle Costlier on Hills Public Land." *Rapid City Journal,* 15 December 1984, pp. 1,2.

————. "Hills Cash Flow Last Among 122 Forests." *Rapid City Journal,* 19 May 1985, pp. 1,2.

————. "Hills May Get Two More Strip Mines." *Rapid City Journal,* 18 January 1985, pp. 1,2.

————. "Homestake Is Granted Permit to Strip Mine." *Rapid City Journal,* 19 July 1984, p 3.

————. "Rancher Says Mining Reclamation Won't Be Easy." *Rapid City Journal,* 8 December 1984, pp. 1,2.

————. "State Minerals Board Dismisses Wharf Mining Application." *Rapid City Journal,* 17 August 1985, p. 1.

————. "Two New Parking Areas to Be Built at Sheridan Lake to Reduce Hazard." *Rapid City Journal,* 9 June 1985, p. 3.

————. "Wharf Needs Expansion to Keep its Golden Eggs in Hills Basket." *Rapid City Journal,* 22 December 1985, sec. A, p. 2.

Miller, David B. "An Essay on the Bradley Bill" — S.705. Rapid City: Rapid City Public Library Vertical Files, undated (circa 1986) .

————. Personal Interview. 9 July 1992.

————. "South Dakota Economic History." Edited by Herbert T. Hoover, 150–60. *Planning for the South Dakota Centennial: A Bibliography.* Brookings: S.D. State University, 1984.

Miller, David J. "Survey is Monument to Stream's Inability". *Pioneer Times,* 11 September 1971, p. 1.

Miller, Steve. "Stories differ on cancellation of Sun Dance." *Rapid City Journal,* 26 July 1973, p. 2.

Milton, John. *South Dakota: A Bicentennial History.* New York: W. W. Norton & Company, 1977.

"Milwaukee Asks to Quit Rapid City". *Rapid City Journal,* 16 July 1951, p. 2.

Miser, Walter G. "South Dakota Mining Law." Francis C. Lincoln, Walter G. Miser, and Joseph B. Cummings. *The Mining Industry of South Dakota.* Rapid City: South Dakota School of Mines, 1937. Bulletin No. 17:44–60.

Modde, T., Henry G. Drewes, and Mark A. Rumble. "Effects of Watershed Alteration on the Brook Trout Population of a Small Black Hills Stream." *Great Basin Naturalist* 46.1 (1986):39–45.

"Moody Letter." *Rapid City Journal,* 7 April 1897, p. 1.

Moody, Sid. "Wilderness: A Key to Survival?" *Rapid City Journal,* 21 April 1968, p. 27.

Morrell, Warren. "Thru the Hills with Warren Morrell." *Rapid City Journal,* 12 December 1946 p. 1.

"Multiple Use Management." *Rapid City Journal,* 20 September 1970, p. 38.

Myers, Charles A. *Simulating the Management of Even-aged Timber Stands.* USDA Forest Service Research Paper RM- 42. Fort Collins, Colo.: Rocky Mountain Forest and Range Experiment Station, 1969.

————. "Natural Thinning of Ponderosa Pine in the Black Hills." *Journal of Forestry,* December (1960):962–64.

———— and Van Deusen, James L. "Site Index of Ponderosa Pine in the Black Hills Form Soil and Topography". *Journal of Forestry,* July (1960):552–55.

National Forest Products Association. "The Monongahela Issue: A Spreading Economic Malady", Supplement to *Hill City Prevailer,* 18 March 1976.

Nauman, Talli. "Nemo Mining Plans Elicit Residents' Concerns." *Rapid City Journal,* 4 June 1979, pp. 1,2.

————. "Newly Formed Black Hills Alliance Committed to Preservation of the Hills." *Rapid City Journal,* 25 February 1979, p. 3

Neel, H. C. and C. W. Fitzgerald. *Report on the Proposed Jewel Cave Game Preserve, Black Hills National Forest, Custer City, S.D.* Custer, S.D.: Black Hills National Forest Historic Files, 1907

Neely, Judy. "Granting of Uranium Exploration Permit Draws Fire from Black Hills Alliance." *Rapid City Journal,* 16 June 1979, p. 3.

————. "Uranium Mining Controversy No Nearer Solution." *Rapid City Journal,* 13

July 1979, p. 1.

Nelson, Paula M. *After the West Was Won: Homesteaders and Town-Builders in Western South Dakota, 1900–1917.* Iowa City: Iowa University Press, 1986.

Nelson, Robert H. "Mythology Instead of Analysis: The Story of Public Forest Management." Edited by Robert T. Deacon, and M. Bruce Johnson. *Forestlands.* San Fransciso: Pacific Institute for Public Policy Research, 1985.

"The New Forest Supervisor." *Rapid City Journal,* 10 September 1898, p. 1.

Newby, Floyd L. "Environmental Impact Appraisal of Proposed Developments in the Harney Peak Area of the Black Hills.", prepared for U.S.Forest Service, Custer, S.D.: Black Hills National Forest Historic Files, (undated, circa mid-1960s).

Newport, Carl A. *Forest Service Policies in Timber Management and Silviculture as They Affect the Lumber Industry: A Case Study of the Black Hills.* Pierre, S.D.: Department of Game, Fish, and Parks, 1956.

Newton, Henry, and Walter Jenney. *Report on the Geology and Resources of the Black Hills of Dakota.* Washington, D.C.: Government Printing Office, 1880.

Nordwall, Donald. (forest supervisor). Letter to Division Chiefs in USFS, BHNF re: plywood plant possibilities. 7 August 1964. Custer, S.D.:Black Hills National Forest, Historic Files.

———. Letter to Senator Karl Mundt re: response to opposition to Harney Peak development. 6 April 1970. Custer, S.D.:Black Hills National Forest, Historic Files.

———. Letter to Senator George McGovern confirming rejection of Harney Peak development plan in light of local opposition. 18 June 1970. Custer, S.D.: Black Hills National Forest Historic Files.

O'Gara, Hugh. "Forest Service, Signs Don't Mix." *Rapid City Journal,* 12 November 1978, p. 2.

———. "Hills Counties Receive Largest Part of Federal Funds in West River Area." *Rapid City Journal,* 24 April 1979, p. 2.

———. "Hills Road Case May Go Beyond U.S. District Court." *Rapid City Journal,* 16 June 1979, p. 2.

———. "Lakota Spiritual Camp Has Temporary Home." *Rapid City Journal,* 1 June 1979, p. 2.

"Oil and Minerals Are Significant." *Rapid City Journal,* 25 April 1976 p. 11.

Orlove, Benjamin S. "The Tragedy of the Commons Revisited: Land Use and Environmental Quality in High Altitude Andean grasslands." Edited by J. Luchok. *Hill Lands.* Proceedings of an International Symposium, Morgantown, West Virginia, 3–6 October 1976. Morgantown: University of West Virginia, 1976.

Orr, Howard K. "Precipitation and Streamflow in the Black Hills." Station Paper No. 44. Fort Collins, Colo.: Rocky Mountain Forest and Range Experiment Station, 1959.

———. "Soil Porosity and Bulk Density on Grazed and Protected Kentucky Bluegrass Range in the Black Hills." *Journal of Range Management* 13.2 (1960):80–86.

———. Letter to Forest Service, Custer re: use of Pine Creek area for research. March 10, 1966. Custer, S.D.: Black Hills National Forest, Historic Files.

———. "Runoff and Erosion Control by Seeded and Native Vegetation on a Forest Burn: Black Hills, South Dakota." USDA Forest Service Research Paper RM-60. Fort Collins,Colo: Rocky Mountain Forest and Range Experiment Station, 1970.

———. "Throughfall and Stemflow Relationships in Second-Growth Ponderosa Pine in the Black Hills." USDA Forest Service Research Note RM-210. Fort Collins, Colo: Rocky Mountain Forest and Range Management Experiment Station, 1972.

———. "The Black Hills (South Dakota) Flood of June 1972: Impacts and Implications." USDA Forest Service General Technical Report RM-2. Fort Collins, Colo.: Rocky Mountain Forest and Range Experiment Station, 1972.

———. "Watershed Management in the Black Hills: The Status or Our Knowledge." USDA Forest Service Research Paper RM-141. Fort Collins, Colo: Rocky Mountain Forest and Range Experiment Station, 1975.

——— and T. VanderHeide. "Water Yield Characteristic of Three Small Watersheds in the Black Hills of South Dakota." USDA Forest Service Research Paper RM-100. Fort Collins,Colo.: Rocky Mountain Forest and Range Experiment Station, 1973.

Ostrom, Elinor. *Governing the Commons: The Evolution of Institutions for Collective Action*. New York: Cambridge University Press, 1991.

———. "Issues of Definition and Theory: Some Conclusions and Hypotheses" in Proceedings of the Conference on Common Property Resource Management, Washington, D.C., 16–21 April 1985.

———. "Constituting Social Capital and Collective Action." *Journal of Theoretical Politics* 6.4(1994):535–67.

O'Toole, Randal. *Reforming the Forest Service*. Washington, D.C.: Island Press, 1988.

———. "At Issue: What's Really Driving National Forest Management?" *American Forests* (Jan./Feb. 1989):58.

"Outlook Favorable For New Lumber Operation in Hills." *Rapid City Journal,* 24 May 1979, p. 1,2.

Palais, Hyman. "The Cattle Industry in the Black Hills." *The Black Hills Engineer* 27.1(1942):1–52.

———. "History of Sheep Raising in the Black Hills." *The Black Hills Engineer* 27.1(1942):53–60.

Parker, Watson. "A Black Hills Bibliography." *South Dakota Historical Collections* XXXV (1970):173–301.

———. *Deadwood, The Golden Years*. Lincoln, Nebr.: University of Nebraska Press, 1981.

———. *Gold in the Black Hills*. Lincoln, Nebr.: University of Nebraska Press, 1966.

Parsons, James. "Will New Roads Spoil the Black Hills?" *Minneapolis Tribune Picture* 21 November 1971: 22–30.

Payne, James W., and Leslie A. Gross, Midland Cultural Development Corporation. "Proposal for Special Use Permit: Black Hills National Forest—Harney Peak and Environs." 6 November 1969. Custer, S.D.: Black Hills National Forest Historic Files.

Peattie, Roderick. *The Black Hills*. New York: Vanguard Press, 1952.

Peet, Richard, and Nigel Thrift. "Political Economy and Human Geography." Edited by Richard Peet and Nigel Thrift, 3–29. *New Models in Geography: The Political Economy Perspective*. London: Unwin Hyman, 1989.

Peterson, R. M. Letter to Charles Fast Horse denying special-use permit. 6 June 1980. Custer, S.D.: Black Hills National Forest Historic Files.

Pilcher, R. J. Letter to Donald Nordwall, USFS re: opposition to Harney Peak development. March 31, 1970. Custer, S.D.: Black Hills National Forest, Historic Files.

Pinchot, Gifford. Breaking New Ground. New York: Harcourt Brace & Co., 1947.

Planke, Max. "Uranium Case Goes to Judge." *Rapid City Journal,* 20 February 1980, p. 2.

"Please Help Preserve Harney Peak in Its Natural State!" *Rapid City Journal,* 18 May 1970, p. 5.

Poffenberger, Mark. *Keepers of the Forests.* West Hartford, Conn.: Kumarian Press, 1990.

Price, Overton W. Letter to Regional Forester re: research value of Upper Pine Creek. 2 September 1966. Custer, S.D.:Black Hills National Forest Historic Files.

Progulske, Donald R. *Yellow Ore, Yellow Hair, Yellow Pine: A Photographic Study of a Century of Forest Ecology.* (Bulletin 616). Brookings, S.D.: South Dakota State University, 1974.

"Prosperity Returning." *Rapid City Journal,* 13 October 1898, p. 1.

"Public Uproar Over Forest Reserve." *Rapid City Journal,* 3 March 1897, p. 1.

Pulling, Hazel A. "History of the Range Cattle Industry of Dakota." *South Dakota Historical Collections.* (Pierre,S.D.: State Historical Society, 1940), 467–521.

"A Question Raised." *Rapid City Journal,* 2 March 1897, p. 1.

"The Range War." *Rapid City Journal,* 31 December 1898, p. 1.

Rapid City Journal. 1890–1985. Published at Rapid City, South Dakota. Available on microfilm, Rapid City Public Library.

Ratliff, Mark R. Letter to Forest Supervisor re: use of forest for stock. 12 September 1941. Custer, S.D.:Black Hills National Forest Historic Files.

———. Letter to O.P.Huney re cutting timber of mining claim. 15 April 1941. Custer, S.D.:Black Hills National Forest Historic Files.

"Reaction Mixed on Hills Claim Interest Ruling." *Rapid City Journal,* 14 June 1979, p. 6.

Rebbeck, Dick. "Aspen Cutting Halts for Study." *Rapid City Journal,* 24 June 1966, p. 1,2.

———. "Aspen Cutting Spurs Browse Production as Pines Get Start." *Rapid City Journal,* 21 September 1969, p. 38.

———. "Bulk of Recreation Fees to Come Back to States." *Rapid City Journal,* 11 April 1965, p. 17.

———. "Congressmen Hear About Loggers' Problems." *Rapid City Journal,* 13 October 1985, p. 2.

———. "Conservation Costs Soaring." *Rapid City Journal,* 25 November 1979, p. 3.

———. "Controversial Proposals Deleted From Study of Black Hills Water Quality Management." *Rapid City Journal,* 28 January 1976, p. 2.

———. "Crook . . . a Superlative County." *Rapid City Journal,* 25 April 1976, p. 11.

———. "Crowded Pines to be Thinned." *Rapid City Journal,* 16 March 1974, p. 11.

———. "Forest Programs Often Benefit From Criticism, Ranger Says." *Rapid City Journal,* 26 April 1980, pp. 1,2.

———. "Forest Service Will Clarify Controversial Grazing Issue." *Rapid City Journal,* 22 January 1982, p. 2.

———. "Grazing Benefits Economy, Land Management." *Rapid City Journal,* 18 June 1982, p. 2.

———. "Grazing District Hearing Enters Third Day." *Rapid City Journal,* 3 May 1963, p. 1.

———. "Harney Wilderness Endorsed." *Rapid City Journal,* 6 April 1972 pp. 1,2.

———. "Headwaters Come Alive Again." *Rapid City Journal,* 5 November 1967, p. 17.

———. "Hearing Held on Proposed Dumont Dam, Lake." *Rapid City Journal,* 25 March 1975, p. 2.

————. "Hills Forest Potential 'Showcase'." *Rapid City Journal,* 21 February 1976, sec.S, p. 10.

————. "Hills Economy Hurt by Sagging Sawmill Industry." *Rapid City Journal,* 11 August 1985, p. 9.

————. "Hills Residents Hit Trail to Get Facts in Controversy Over Aspen." *Rapid City Journal,* 20 June 1966, p. 2.

————. "Hills Water 'Has Lost Ground'." *Rapid City Journal,* 3 October 1975, p. 2.

————. "Homestake Won't Rebuild in Spearfish." *Rapid City Journal,* 14 May 1980, p. 1,2.

————. "Impacts of Mining Seem to 'Sneak Up'." *Rapid City Journal,* 13 April 1975, p. 1,2.

————. "Interest High in 'Copter Logging Project." *Rapid City Journal,* 23 February 1974, p. 2.

————. "Land Shows Scars of 'Aspen War'." *Rapid City Journal,* 31 August 1969, p. 39.

————. "Land Use Begins to Emerge as a Major State Controversy." *Rapid City Journal,* 23 February 1974, sec. A pp.3–4.

————. "Lien Future Is Bright." *Rapid City Journal,* 18 May 1967, p. 16.

————. "Local Input on Mining Important." *Rapid City Journal,* 15 April 1975, p. 1.

————. "Local Logging Industry Situation Couldn't Be Much Worse." *Rapid City Journal,* 6 May 1980, p. 2.

————. "Logging Was Essential to Black Hills Mining." *Rapid City Journal,* 24 May 1976, p. 11.

————. "Lumber Industry Expects Better Year in 1981." *Rapid City Journal,* 28 February 1981, sec. S, p. 19.

————. "Mining Tax Revenue Benefit Performance Isn't Convincing." *Rapid City Journal,* 14 April 1975, p. 1,2.

————. "Pay-to-play in Hills Defended." *Rapid City Journal,* 19 May 1965, p. 1.

————. "Planned Destruction of Aspen Draws Fire." *Rapid City Journal,* 10 June 1966, p. 1,2.

————. "Private Operator Will Run Forest Service Concessions." *Rapid City Journal,* 11 April 1982, p. 3.

————. "Simple Answer Rare in Seeking to Define Hills Resource Need." *Rapid City Journal,* 14 January 1968, p. 15.

————. "Sans Fireworks, Public Land Accord Possible During 1963." *Rapid City Journal,* 26 December 1962, p. 3.

————. "Significant Energy Role Seen for Forests." *Rapid City Journal,* 15 May 1981, p. 2.

————. "Spring, Rapid Creek Pollution Is Serious." *Rapid City Journal,* 20 December 1969, p. 1.

————. "Straw Vote Strongly Favors Sheridan Lake As It Is." *Rapid City Journal,* 27 March 1973, p. 2.

————. "Strip Mine Case Bodes S.D. Water Law Test." *Rapid City Journal,* 4 March 1962, p. 21.

————. "They Call Bombing Range Home." *Rapid City Journal,* 20 July 1969, p. 3.

————. "Tighter Fuel Wood Management Possible." *Rapid City Journal,* 1 November 1981, p. 1–2.

————. "Timber, Grass Management May Be Key to Water Conservation." *Rapid City*

Journal, 31 July 1961, p. 1.

———. "Timber Management, Beef Production Have Strong Link." *Rapid City Journal,* 12 April 1981, p. 2.

———. "Timber Marketing Outlook Optimistic." *Rapid City Journal,* 23 February 1980, sec.S, p. 26.

———. "Timber Plan Charts Hills Future." *Rapid City Journal,* 10 April 1976, p. 13.

———. "Time to Ask Questions About Mining." *Rapid City Journal,* 7 April 1975, p. 1.

———. "Vehicle Use Guidelines Proposed." *Rapid City Journal,* 7 July 1974, p. 1,2.

———. "Washington Seems to Be Hearing Hills Timber Industry's SOS message." *Rapid City Journal,* 15 November 1985, p. 1.

———. "Water in a Nose Dive." *Rapid City Journal,* 10 November 1965, p. 29.

———. "Wildland Status Sentiment Evident for Harney." *Rapid City Journal,* 5 April 1972, p. 1.

Reed, C. Letter to B. Lloyd re: Roughlock Nature Trail. 16 June 1965. Custer, S.D.: Black Hills National Forest Historic Files.

Rees, Judith. *Natural Resources: Allocation, Economics and Policy.* New York: Routledge, 1990.

Relph, Edward. "Phenomenology." Edited by M. E. Harvey, and Brian P. Holly, 99–114. *Themes in Geographic Thought.* New York: St. Martin's Press, 1981.

Repetto, Robert. *The Global Possible.* New Haven, Conn.: Yale University Press, 1985.

——— and Thomas Holmes. "The Role of Population in Resource Depletion in Developing Countries." *Population and Development Review* 9.4 (1983):609–32.

Rezatto, Hazel. *Tales of the Black Hills.* Rapid City, S.D.: Fenwyn Press, 1989.

Riley, L. Letter to Chief Forester re: condition of Bear Lodge National Forest. 1 July 1907. Custer, S.D.: Black Hills National Forest, Historic Files.

Riley, Marvin. "State Biggest Population Problem: How Can You Keep Them Home?" *Rapid City Journal,* 13 February 1961, p. 3.

Riley, Paul. "Beaver Park Walk Shows Little Signs of Wildlife." *Rapid City Journal,* 23 March 1979, sec. V. p. 3.

———. "Benchmark Area Roads, Trees to Be Cut Down." *Rapid City Journal,* 12 November 1978, p. 31.

———. "Black Hills Party Debris Brings Growing Forest Service Problem." *Rapid City Journal,* 4 January 1980, p. 3.

———. "Black Hills May Have More Roads, Not Fewer." *Rapid City Journal,* 15 February 1979, p. 2.

———. "Century-Old Flume Becoming Hiking Trail." *Rapid City Journal,* 27 April 1979, sec. V, p. 3.

———. "Custer Landowner Fighting Forest Service Road Plan." *Rapid City Journal,* 16 October 1978, pp. 1,2.

———. "David Miller and David Miller: Remarkable Similarities." *Rapid City Journal,* 18 March 1980, p. 11.

———. "Do the Black Hills Need More Trees?" *Rapid City Journal,* 3 September 1978, p. 27.

———. "Everyone and Everything Benefits." *Rapid City Journal,* 8 September 1978, sec. V, p. 3.

———. "Feeding Aspen Could Be Easier and Cheaper." *Rapid City Journal,* 14 October 1977, p. 9.

———. "Forest Road Plans Inadequately Aired." *Rapid City Journal*, 13 January 1980, p. 3.

———. "Forest Service Begins Three-Year Plan to Close 900 Miles of Roads." *Rapid City Journal*, 3 October 1979, p. 38.

———. "Forest Service Defines Difference Between Roadless and Wilderness Areas." *Rapid City Journal*, 23 August 1977, p. 3.

———. "Forest Service Funds Wildlife Habitat Projects." *Rapid City Journal*, 11 August 1978, sec. V, p. 3.

———. "Forest Service Official Says Wildlife Has Equality." *Rapid City Journal*, 8 April 1979, p. 2.

———. "Forest Service Sets Open Houses for Public Input Into Wilderness Planning." *Rapid City Journal*, 27 June 1978, p. 2.

———. "GF&P Official Concerned About Future of Hills Game Populations." *Rapid City Journal*, 12 February 1977, p. 13.

———. "Grazing Interests Ask Extension of Time for Comments on Land Use." *Rapid City Journal*, 28 August 1977, p. 1.

———. "Hills Use Pattern Changing." *Rapid City Journal*, 23 February 1980, sec. S, p. 29.

———. "Landowners Plan Suit Over Pollution Problems." *Rapid City Journal*, 21 April 1978, p. 1.

———. "Mining Discussion Fails to Answer All Questions." *Rapid City Journal*, 9 August 1979, p. 1,2.

———. "No One Knows Why Black Hills Deer Declining." *Rapid City Journal*, 17 June 1977, p. 8.

———. "Quality First Concern in Pactola Recreation Plan." *Rapid City Journal*, 26 September 1978, p. 2.

———. "Sioux Denied Site for Spiritual Camp Near Custer." *Rapid City Journal*, 17 July 1979, p. 2.

———. "Site of Indian Spiritual Camp Remains at Issue." *Rapid City Journal*, 1 October 1979, p. 1.

———. "Spearfish Takes Lead in Aspen Management." *Rapid City Journal*, 18 April 1980, sec. V, p. 3.

———. "Trout Population Increases While Their Habitat Decreases." *Rapid City Journal*, 14 December 1979, sec. V, p. 3.

———. "Two-track Trails Disappearing." *Rapid City Journal*, 8 January 1978, p. 23.

———. "U.S. Forest Service to Spend $542,000 to Expand, Improve Area Campgrounds." *Rapid City Journal*, 17 August 1977, p. 1.

———. "Wilderness Area Rates High for Mineral Potential." *Rapid City Journal*, 17 January 1979, p. 1.

Ritter, Michael. "Coal, Uranium Could Draw Thousands." *Rapid City Journal*, 2 June 1980, p. 13.

———. "Edgemont Yard Cleanup Would Cost $108,000." *Rapid City Journal*, 30 July 1980, p. 2.

———. "Union Carbide Makes Threat of Pullout." *Rapid City Journal*, 4 April 1980, p. 1.

Rountree, Lester B. and Margaret W. Conkey. "Symbolism and the Cultural Landscape." *Annals of the Association of American Geographers* 70.4 (1980): 459–74.

Rumble, Mark A. "Biota of Uranium Mill Tailings Near the Black Hills." Proceedings of the Annual Conference of the Western Association of Fish and Wildlife Agencies, 18–22 July 1982, Las Vegas.

———. "Radiation Dosimetry on Revegetated Uranium Tailings in Western South Dakota." *Northwest Science* 60.3 (1986):145–49.

———. "Surface Mine Impoundments as Wildlife and Fish Habitat." USDA Forest Service General Technical Report RM-183. Fort Collins, Colo: Rocky Mountain Forest and Range Experiment Station, 1989.

———. "Wildlife Associated with Scoria Outcrops: Implications for Reclamation of Surface-mined Lands." USDA Forest Service Research Paper RM-285. Fort Collins, Colo.: Rocky Mountain Forest and Range Experiment Station, 1989.

———. and A. J. Bjugstad. "Uranium and Radium Concentrations in Plants Growing on Uranium Mill Tailings in South Dakota." *Reclamation and Revegetation Research* 4(1986):271–277.

Rupp, Craig. Letter to Charles Fast Horse denying appeal of special use permit for spiritual camp. 2 November 1979. Custer, S.D.: Black Hills National Forest, Historic Files.

Russell, D. Letter to Director, Black Hills National Forest re: opposition to Harney Peak Development. 13 May 1970. Custer, S.D.: Black Hills National Forest, Historic Files.

Russell, J. Letter to Senator Karl Mundt re: Opposition to Harney Peak development. 15 May 1970. Custer, S.D.:Black Hills National Forest Historic Files.

Sample, Al. "At Issue: What's Really Driving National Forest Mangaement?" *American Forests* (Jan./Feb.1989):58.

Schallau, Don H. "Community Stability: Issues, Institutions, and Instruments." Edited by Robert G. Lee, Donald R. Field, and J. William Burch,Jr., 69–82. *Community and Forestry.* Boulder, Colo: Westview Press, 1990.

Scherrer, Bertha, and Ellen Mohr. "Newcastle Enjoys New Oil Boom, but It Strains City Facilities, Schools." *Rapid City Journal,* 17 January 1954, p. 5.

Schlager, Edella, and Elinor Ostrom. "Property-Rights Regimes and Natural Resources: A Conceptual Analysis" *Land Economics* 68.3 (1992): 249–62.

Schlapfer, T.H.Letter to Regional Forester re: plywood plant possibilities. 17 August 1964. Custer, S.D.: Black Hills National Forest, Historic Files.

——— and J. H. Lombard. "Memorandum of Understanding between the United States Forest Service, Department of Agriculture and the National Park Service, Department of Interior" (regarding Jewel Cave development). 9 February 1965. Custer, S.D.: Black Hills National Forest, Historic Files.

Schneeweis, J. C. and T. E.Schenck. *Food Habits of Deer in the Black Hills.* Bulletin 606. Brookings, S.D.: Agricultural Experiment Station, South Dakota State University, 1972.

Schneider, Peter. "Logging Can Benefit Hills Groundwater." *Rapid City Journal,* 9 November 1980, p. 2.

———. "Sheridan Lake Dam Upgrading to Cost $250,000." *Rapid City Journal,* 25 August 1980, p. 2.

Schnute, D. Letter to Senator McGovern re: opposition to Harney Peak development. 21 March 1970. Custer, S.D.:Black Hills National Forest, Historic Files.

Scholz, Kenneth C. Letter to Regional Forester, Denver re: transfer of Deerfield Reservoir. 17 January 1967. Custer, S.D.:Black Hills National Forest, Historic Files.

————. Letter to Regional Forester, Denver, re: Harney Peak development. 23 June 1967. Custer, S.D.: Black Hills National Forest, Historic Files.

Schrader, F.C. *Report on the Jewel and Four Other Lode Claims.* 15 April 1909. Custer, S.D.;: Black Hills National Forest Historic Files.

"Second Census of South Dakota, 1905." *South Dakota Public Documents.* Aberdeen, S.D.: News Printing Co., 1905.

Sedjo, Roger A. *Governmental Interventions, Social Needs, and the Management of U.S. Forests.* Washington, D.C.: Resources for the Future, 1983.

"Selling Multiple Use Management," Forest Service conference held at Black Hills National Forest. 6–10 June 1960. Custer, S.D.:Black Hills National Forest, Historic Files.

"Senator Pettigrew." *Rapid City Journal,* 11 August 1898, p. 1.

Severson, Kieth E. "Production and Nutritive Value of Aspen Understory, Black Hills." *Journal of Range Management* 35.6 (1982):786–89.

————. "Options for Black Hills Forest Owners: Timber, Forage, or Both." *Rangeman's Journal* 4.1 (1977):13–5.

————. "Cattle, Wildlife, and Riparian Habitats in the Western Dakotas." *Management and use of Northern Plains Rangeland,* Proceedings of Regional Rangeland Symposium, Bismarck, N.D., 27–28 February, 1978.

———— and Charles E. Boldt. "Problems Associated with Management of Native Woody Plants in the Western Dakotas." Edited by K.L. Johnson. *Wyoming Shrublands.* 1977. Proceedings of the Sixth Wyoming Shrub Ecology Workshop, Buffalo, WY, 24–25 May 1977.

———— and F. R. Gartner. "Problems in Commercial Hunting Systems: South Dakota and Texas Compared." *Journal of Range Management* 25 (1972):342–45.

———— and J. J. Krantz. "Management of Bur Oak on Deer Winter Range". *The Wildlife Society Bulletin* 6.4 (1978):212–16.

———— and J. F. Thilenius. *Classification of Quaking Aspen Stands in the Black Hills and Bear Lodge Mountains.* USDA Forest Service Research Paper RM-166. Fort Collins, Colo.: Rocky Mountain Forest and Range Experiment Station, 1976.

Seyhers, L., T. L. Clausen and L. Parsons. Letters to the Editor. *Rapid City Journal,* 21 May 1970, p. 5.

Shepherd, Jack. *The Forest Killers.* New York: Weybright and Talley, 1975.

Shepperd, Wayne D., and Sue E. McElderry. "Ten-Year Results of a Ponderosa Pine Progeny Test in the Black Hills." *Western Journal of Applied Forestry* 1.3 (1986):79–83.

Sheridan, Thomas. *Where the Dove Calls: The Political Ecology of a Peasant Corporate Community in Northwestern Mexico.* Tucson: University of Arizona Press, 1988.

Singsaas, Eugene B. "The Future of the Concession Program on the Black Hills National Forest". Custer, S.D.: Black Hills National Forest, Supervisor's Office, 1987.

————. Personal Interview. 17 November 1992.

"Sioux Get Temporary Spiritual Camp." *Queen City Mail,* 6 June 1979, p. 9.

"Sitting Bull's Grandson Still Fighting For His Tribe." *Rocky Mountain News,* 28 September, 1980, p. 1.

Sittner, James A. *Multiple Use Conflicts in the Black Hills of South Dakota and Wyoming.* Master's Thesis. Rapid City, S.D.: South Dakota School of Mines and Technology, 1970.

Sixth District Council of Local Governments. *Economic Diversification: "A Primer For Economic Change."* Rapid City, S.D.: Sixth District Council of Local Governments, 1976.

Skie, Morrie. "The Ikes and pollution." *Rapid City Journal,* 29 April 1970, p. 11.

Smith, Frank E. *Conservation in the United States: Land and Water 1900–1970.* New York: Chelsea House Publishers, 1971.

Smith, Richard C., William B. Kurtz, and Thomas E. Johnson. "Cost Efficiency of Pruning Black Hills Ponderosa Pine." *Western Journal of Applied Forestry* 3.1 (1988): 10–14.

"Some Facts and Figures about the Black Hills." *Rapid City Journal,* 27 January 1897, p 1. (repeated weekly through 1899).

Sorensen, T. Letter to Senator Karl Mundt re: opposition to Harney Peak development. 16 March 1970. Custer, S.D.: Black Hills National Forest, Historic Files.

South Dakota. "Agricultural Statistics." *1905 Public Documents South Dakota;* Aberdeen, S.D.: News Printing Co., 1905.

―――. Department of Highways. *Preliminary Tabulations of Selected Data from Returned Questionnaires, Black Hills Area Transportation Study.* Custer, S.D.: Black Hills National Forest, Historic Files, 1972.

―――. Office of Executive Management. *South Dakota Facts: An Abstract of Statistics and Graphics Concerning People and Resources of South Dakota.* Pierre, S.D.: State Planning Bureau, 1976.

―――. State Planning Board. *Land Ownership in South Dakota as of March 1, 1934.* Brookings, S.D.: State Planning Board, 1937.

―――. "Mining Directory of South Dakota." Edited by Walter G. Miser and Joseph B. Cummings. *The Mining Industry of South Dakota.* Bulletin No. 17:61–167. Rapid City, S.D.: South Dakota School of Mines, 1940.

"South Dakota Leads Western States in Proportionate Increase in Lumber." *Rapid City Journal,* 4 November 1978, P. 16.

"Spearfish Forest Service Office to Close." *Queen City Mail,* 11 September 1969, P. 1.

Spencer, J. Letter to Chief Forester re: naming of consolidated forest. 23 December 1946. Custer, S.D.:Black Hills National Forest, Historic Files.

"Statute Regarding Receipts to States from Forests." Act of May 23, 1908, 35 Stat. 250, Section 500, Title 16 United States Code and Act of June 30, 1914 (38 Stat 441).

Steen, Henry K. *Origins of the National Forests: A Centenniel Symposium.* Durham, N.C.: Forest History Society, 1992.

Stevenson, Glenn G. *Common Property Economics.* New York: Cambridge University Press, 1991.

Sullivan, Maureen. "Final Decision on Black Hills Interest in Hands of Supreme Court." *Rapid City Journal,* 14 April 1980, p. 1,2.

Sundstrom, Jessie Y., and Carl H. Sundstrom. *Custer County History to 1976.* Custer, S.D.: Custer County Historical Society, 1977.

Taylor, Kay. "Daschle Discusses Proposed User Fees at Sheridan Lake Meeting". *Rapid City Journal,* 9 June 1985, p. 3.

―――. "Wilderness Revives the Soul." *Rapid City Journal,* 19 February 1978, p. 25.

"Temporary Permit Issued Spiritual Camp." *Hot Springs Star,* 6 June 1979, p. 6.

"Temporary Permit Not Accepted by Indians." *Custer County Chronicle,* 7 June 1979, p. 1.

"Ten Year Forestry Plan Released." *Hill City (S.D.) Prevailer,* 15 April 1976, Special Forest Products Section, p. 3.

Thilenius, John F. 1972. *Classification of Deer Habitat in the Ponderosa Pine Forest of the Black Hills, South Dakota.* USDA Forest Service Research Paper RM-91. Fort Collins,Colo: Rocky Mountain Forest and Range Experiment Station, 1972.

Third Census of South Dakota, 1915. Sioux Falls: Press of Mark D. Scott, 1915.

"Those Timber Cases." *Rapid City Journal,* 22 January 1898, p. 1.

Timber Application File. 1898–1925. Custer, S.D.:Black Hills National Forest Historic File.

"Timber Management Keeps Hills Green." *Queen City Mail,* 4 July 1968, p. 1.

Todaro, Michael P. *Economic Development in the Third World,* 4th Ed., New York: Longman, 1987.

Troendle, Carl A. "Effect of Partial Cutting and Thinning on the Water Balance of the Subalpine Forest." *Journal of Range Management* 31.6 (1978): 439–42.

Tuan, Yi-Fu. "Sacred Space: Explorations of an Idea." Edited by Karl Butzer. *Dimensions of Human Geography.* University of Chicago Research Paper 186. 1978.

Tucker, Bob. "Battle of Gold Tax Fought; War Not Over." *Rapid City Journal,* 5 February 1981, p. 1,2.

———. "Hunt for Precious Metals Thriving in Hills." *Rapid City Journal,* 8 June 1981, p. 1,2.

———. "Indian Land Ownership at Issue in Suit." *Rapid City Journal,* 27 March 1982, p. 1,2.

———. "State Ready to Fight Sioux Hills Claim Suit." *Rapid City Journal,* 29 August 1980, p. 1.

———. "Union Carbide Given Exploration Permit." *Rapid City Journal,* 10 April 1981, p. 2.

Turner, R. Kerry. *Sustainable Environmental Management.* Boulder, Colo: Westview Press, 1988.

Tuttle, Tom. "Barren Hillsides Mark Revival of Open Cut Mining Project." *Rapid City Journal,* 8 November 1983, p. 3.

"United States v. Means." United States District Court Case, District of South Dakota. 627 Federal Supplement, 1985, 247–72.

United States Bureau of Reclamation. *Report to Forest Service on activity at Deerfield Reservoir.* Billings, Mont: Bureau of Reclamation, 1967.

———. Department of Agriculture. "Regulations Governing Applications Under the Act of June 11, 1906." Custer, S.D.: Black Hills National Forest, Historic Files.

———. ———. *Silviculture Systems for the Major Forest Types of the United States.* USDA Handbook 445. Washington, DC: Government Printing Office, 1973.

———. ———. 1905–1985. *Yearbook of Agriculture.* Washington,D.C.: Government Printing Office.

———. and United States Department of the Interior (sponsors). *Black Hills Area Resources Study.* Washington, D.C.: Government Printing Office, 1967.

———. ———. *Black Hills Area Resource Conservation and Development Project Plan.* Lincoln, Nebr.: USDA, 1969.

———. ———. Forest Service. Black Hills National Forest. "Homesteads since 1898." Undated (circa 1903). Office memorandum. Custer, S.D.: Black Hills National Forest Historic Files.

————. *Black Hills National Forest Five Year Evaluation of the Forest Plan.* Custer, S.D.: BHNF Supervisor's Office, 1989.

————. Comments on Norbeck Rare II Areas.Undated (circa early 1980s). Custer, S.D.: Black Hills National Forest Historic Files.

————. "Draft Environmental Impact Statement, Norbeck Wildlife Preserve." 1989. Custer, S.D.: Black Hills National Forest Historic Files.

————. Draft "Chapter 4: Forest Plan." Custer, S.D.: U.S.Forest Service, Cultural Resources, 1992.

————. *Final (and Draft) Environmental Impact Statement. Black Hills National Forest, Land and Resource Mangement Plan.* Custer, S.D.: Black Hills National Forest Supervisor's Office, 1981.

————. File Memo re: 10 day rule for camping areas. 23 February 1956. Custer, S.D.: Black Hills National Forest, Historic Files.

————. *Final Environmental Impact Statement.* Norbeck Wildlife Preserve Land Management Plan, Black Hills National Forest. Custer, S.D.: Black Hills National Forest Supervisor's Office, 1979.

————. *Harney National Forest of South Dakota.* 1953. Custer, S.D.:Black Hills National Forest, Historic Files.

————. "Inyan Kara Mountain, National Register of Historic Places Inventory Nomination Form." 27 August 1971. Custer, S.D.:Black Hills National Forest, Historic Files.

————. *Land and Resource Management Plan, Black Hills National Forest.* Custer, S.D.: Black Hills National Forest Supervisor's Office, 1977.

————. *Management Plan Harney Working Circle Black Hills National Forest.* Custer, S.D.: Black Hills National Forest. Historic Files. 1956.

————. *Master Plan for the Protection and Administration of the Norbeck Wildlife Preserve.* Custer, S.D.:Black Hills National Forest, Historic File, 1927.

————. Pactola District. "Rapid Creek Recreational Unit, Black Hills National Forest." *Forest Plan 1931–1932.* Custer, S.D.: Black Hills National Forest, Historic Files.

————. "Plan of Work, Harney and Black Hills National Forests Grazing Use Adjustments". 14 April 1943. Custer, S.D.:Black Hills National Forest Historic Files.

————. *Plan for Handling the Timber Business of the Black Hills and Harney National Forests.* 23 March 1923. Custer, S.D.:Black Hills National Forest Historic Files.

————. *Policy Statement and Timber Sale Plan, Northeast Working Circle, Black Hills National Forest.* Custer, S.D.:Black Hills National Forest Historic File, 1923.

————. *Proposed Land And Resource Management Plan, Black Hills National Forest.* Custer, S.D.: Black Hills National Forest Supervisor's Office, 1976.

————. *RARE II: Draft Environmental Statement Roadless Area Review and Evaluation.* Washington, DC:USDA Forest Service. (and supplements for Wyoming and Central States), 1978.

————. *Report on Mining Claims, Jewel Cave.* Custer, S.D.: Black Hills National Forest, Historic Files, 1908.

————. *Supplement to Rapid City Working Circle Management Plan.* Custer, S.D.: Black Hills National Forest, Historic Files, 1950.

————. *Supplement to Spearfish Working Circle Mananagement Plan.* Custer, S.D.: Black Hills National Forest, Historic Files,1953.

————. *Timber Management Plan Black Hills National Forest 1977–1986.* Custer,

S.D.: BHNF Supervisor's Office, 1977.

————. *Norbeck Unit Management Plan Black Hills National Forest.* Custer: BHNF Supervisor's Office, 1973.

————. and Soil Conservation Service. "Emergency Report on Potential and Existing Flood Hazards and Emergency Remedial Measures for Certain Tributaries of Whitewood Creek, Black Hills National Forest, Deadwood." Custer, S.D.:United States Forest Service, 1959.

————. ————. Rocky Mountain Region. "Photo Series for Quantifying Forest Residues in the Black Hills Pondersoa Type, Spruce Type. Washington, D. C.: Government Printing Office. 1982.

————. ————. Rocky Mountain Region. "Photo Series for Quantifying Forest Residues in the Black Hills Pondersoa Type, Spruce Type. Washington, D.C.: Government Printing Office. 1990.

————. Department of Commerce. Bureau of the Census. *1890- 1980 Census of Population.* Washington, D.C.: Government Printing Office.

————. Public Lands Commission. *Use and Abuse of America's Natural Resources (with Appendix).* Washington, D.C. Government Printing Office. 1880.

————. Senate Committee on Small Business. 1994. One Hundred Third Congress, "First Session on Hearing on Public Land Use Impact on Small Business", 4 September 1993. Washington, D.C.: Government Printing Office.

"Uranium Field Suggests Reason for New Regulations." *Rapid City Journal,* 2 May 1971, p. 1.

"Uranium Possibilities." *Rapid City Journal,* 9 September 1897, p. 1.

Uresk, Daniel W. Personal Interview. 9 November 1992.

————.(editor). *Proceedings of Black Hills Deer Management Workshop* held in Rapid City, S.D., 9–10 January 1980.

————. and Dennis G. Lowrey. "Cattle Diets in the Central Black Hills of South Dakota." Presented at the Symposium on Wooded Draws. South Dakota School of Mines, Rapid City, S.D., 12–13 June 1984.

———— and Wayne W. Painter. "Cattle Diets in a Ponderosa Pine Forest in the Northern Black Hills." *Journal of Range Management* 38.5 (1985):44–42.

Van Deusen, James L. "Five-Year Results of a Ponderosa Pine Provenance Study in the Black Hills." USDA Forest Service Research Note RM-278. Fort Collins, Colo.: Rocky Mountain Forest and Range Experiment Station, 1974.

————. "Periodic Growth of Pole-Sized Ponderosa Pine as Related to Thinning and Selected Environmental Factors." USDA Forest Service Research Paper RM-38. Fort Collins, Colo.: Rocky Mountain Forest and Range Experiment Station, 1968.

———— and C. A. Myers. "Porcupine Damage in Immature Stands of Ponderosa Pine in the Black Hills." *Journal of Forestry* 60.11 (1962):811–13.

Van Haverbeke, D. F. "Root Development of Ponderosa Pine Seedlings in the Black Hills." *Ecology* 44.1 (1963)161- 65.

Von Schrenck, Henry. *The "Bluing" and the "Red Rot" of the Western Yellow Pine, with Special Reference to the Black Hills Forest Reserve.* Washington, D.C.: Government Printing Office, 1903.

Wagner, Robert T., Eugene T. Butler, and Karen A. McComish. *Population projection models for South Dakota, 1980, 1985, and 1990.* Brookings: Agricultural Experiment Station, South Dakota State University, 1975.

Warren, C. J. "The Manufacture of Black Hils Forest Products." *The Black Hills Engineer* 16.2 (1928):135–46.

Watson, N. F. Memo to Forest Supervisor re: use of Sheridan Lake. 18 August 1947. Custer, S.D.: Black Hills National Forest, Historic Files.

Webster, C. B. "Management Plan for Custer Working Circle, Harney National Forest, South Dakota." Inman F. Eldredge, *Management Plans with Special Reference to the National Forests*. Washington, D.C.: Government Printing Office, 1928. Miscellaneous Publication No. 11: Appendix. 21–39.

Wedge, Lucille. *Gold gave birth to Hill City, South Dakota: The story of an 1876 gold mining community*. Hill City, S.D.: Hill City Historical Society, 1979.

Weisbeck, Mike. "Yellow Thunder: Striving to Save Tradition." *Rapid City Journal*, 4 April 1982, p. 1.

"What It (Monongahela Court Decision) Means to the Black Hills." *Hill City Prevailer*, 18 March 1976: Special Section, p. 2.

White, Gilbert F. "The Choice of Use in Resource Management." Edited by Robert Kates and Ian Burton, 143–65, Vol. I. *Geography, Resources and Environment*. Chicago: University of Chicago Press, 1986.

———. "Formation and Role of Public Attitudes." Edited by Robert Kates and Ian Burton, 219–45, Vol. I. *Geography, Resources and Environment*. Chicago: University of Chicago Press, 1986.

Whitley, Florence W. "A History of Custer City, South Dakota, 1874–1900." *South Dakota Historical Collections*. (Pierre, S.D.: State Historical Society, 1974.), 234–343.

Williams, Michael. *Americans and their Forests: A Historical Geography*. New York: Cambridge University Press, 1989.

Willis, Dick. "Controversial Sheridan Lake Fee Plan OK'd." *Rapid City Journal*, 25 April 1984, p. 1.

———. "Forest Service Closing Road to Jenney Gulch." *Rapid City Journal*, 9 January 1985, p. 3.

———. "Forest Service Eyeing Hills Water Skiing." *Rapid City Journal*, 13 July 1984, p. 1.

———. "Forest Service, GF&P Disagree Over Effects of Management Plan." *Rapid City Journal*, 20 November 1981, p. 2.

———. "Forest Service May Take Over Much of Line." *Rapid City Journal*, 19 August 1983, p. 2.

———. "Forest Service Says There's No Room Away From It All on Hot Weekends." *Rapid City Journal*, 24 June 1985, p. 3.

———. "Forest Service Seeks Deerfield Lake Input." *Rapid City Journal*, 17 May 1985, sec. V, p. 3.

———. "Forest Service to Thin, Burn More Pine Trees." *Rapid City Journal*, 19 June 1983, p. 2.

———. "Forest Service, Wildlife Group Disagree on Mining in Hills." *Rapid City Journal*, 10 December 1983, p. 1.

———. "GP&F, Forest Service Disagree on Potato Creek's Fate." *Rapid City Journal*, 8 October 1982, sec.V. p. 3.

———. "GF&P, Forest Service Plan to Stock More Bighorn Sheep in Black Hills." *Rapid City Journal*, 10 October 1985, p. 32.

———. "Hills Deer Continue to Lose Valuable Browse." *Rapid City Journal*, 20 November 1981, sec.V, p. 3.

———. "Hills forest becoming a refuse dump." *Rapid City Journal*, 17 December 1984, pp. 1–2.

———. "Hills Group Wants Jobs Bill to Include Timber Thinning." *Rapid City Journal*, 24 February 1983, p. 2.

———. "Iron Creek Lake Fish To Be Killed." *Rapid City Journal*, 7 August 1983, p. 31.

———. "Lake User Fee Critics Blast Forest Service." *Rapid City Journal*, 5 July 1984, p. 3.

———. "Most Sheridan Lake Goers Happy Over Decision to End User Fees." *Rapid City Journal*, 2 August 1984, pp. 1,2.

———. "Officials Rule Management Plan for National Forest Needs Work." *Rapid City Journal*, 17 May 1984, p. 3.

———. "Plans Being Made for Hiking Trail Through Hills." *Rapid City Journal*, 5 April 1985, sec.V, p. 3.

———. "Ranchers Support Forest Service Plan to Cut 'That Weed'." *Rapid City Journal*, 4 December 1981, p. 1.

———. "Senate Bill 842 Termed 'Anti-Wilderness'." *Rapid City Journal*, 3 May 1981: Outdoors Section, p. 38.

———. "Sheridan Fees End; Money Troubles Stay." *Rapid City Journal*, 30 September 1984, pp. 1,2.

———. "Sheridan Lake: Potential Unfulfilled." *Rapid City Journal*, 11 May 1984, sec. V, p. 3.

———. "Sheridan Lake to Have New Look." *Rapid City Journal*, 23 October 1983, p. 37.

———. "Trout Caught in Portion of Stream Must Be Released." *Rapid City Journal*, 26 April 1985, sec. V, p. 3.

———. "Volunteer Work in the Forest Is Up 800%." *Rapid City Journal*, 18 March 1984, p. 1.

———. "Wildlife Group Assails Hills Management Plan." *Rapid City Journal*, 29 November 1983, p. 3.

———. "Wyoming Black Hills a Secluded Place To Just Get Away From It All." *Rapid City Journal*, 4 May 1984, sec. V, p. 3.

Willoughby, Hugh, and C. L. Sowards. "Trout Streams in Hills Regions Vanishing as Habitat Decreases." *Rapid City Journal*, 25 August 1959: Special Soil Conservation Edition.

Wilson, George. "Tree Cutting Takes Priority Under Nixon." *Rapid City Journal*, 19 August 1973, p. 31.

Wilson, John. Letter to Gifford Pinchot transferring the Forest Service to the Department of Agriculture. 1 February 1905. Custer, S.D.:Black Hills National Forest, Historic Files.

"Without Compensation?" *Sturgis Tribune*, 12 December 1979, p. 1.

Woodward, M. H. Letter to Regional Forester re: mineral claim. 22 May 1939. Custer, S.D.:Black Hills National Forest, Historic Files.

Yamamoto, Teruo. "A Review of Uranium Spoil and Mill Tailings Revegetation in the Western United States." USDA Forest Service General Technical Report RM-92. Fort Collins, Colo: Rocky Mountain Forest and Range Experiment Station, 1982.

———— and Howard K. Orr. "Morphometry of Three Small Watersheds, Black Hills, South Dakota, and Some Hydrologic Implications". USDA Forest Service Research Paper RM-93. Fort Collins, Colo: Rocky Mountain Forest and Range Experiment Station, 1972.

Young, Steve. "Black Hills Land Issue Foremost in Minds of Many Sioux." *Rapid City Journal,* 28 August 1985, p. 35.

Zimmerer, Karl. 1991. "Wetland Production and smallholder Persistence: Agricultural Change in a Highland Peruvian Region." *Annals of the Association of American Geographers* 81:443–63.

Zimmerman, Edward W. *World Resources and Industries.* New York: Harper and Collins, 1951.

Zivnuska, John A. "Forestry Investments for Multiple Uses Among Multiple Ownership Types." Edited by Marion Clawson. *Forest Policy for the Future.* Proceedings of Conference. Washington, D.C., 8–9 May 1974.

Index

About the Author

Martha Geores is an assistant professor of geography at the University of Maryland at College Park. She conducted the research for this book during her days as a graduate student in the Department of Geography at the University of North Carolina at Chapel Hill. Her interests in common property resources predate her formal studies of geography and stem from her life in rural Maine and her work as an attorney for natural resources users. Her research interests include natural resource definition, population and environment interactions, and cultural issues which accompany these topics.